# GOTNOPHOBIA

## Progressive, Contagious And Incurable Courage

## Timothy M. Hacker

# DEDICATION

To my Grandson Landon – May God grant to
you, your children, and your children's children
greater and greater levels of freedom from every fear as the
revelation of God's great love fills the earth in your day!

# CONTENTS

FOREWORD....................................................................1

ACKNOWLEDGEMENTS ...........................................5

PREFACE.......................................................................7

INTRODUCTION .........................................................9

1. Taphophobia - Fear of Being Buried Alive ..............11

2. Phobophobia – Fear of Being Afraid.......................27

3. Gigantasophobia – Fear of Giants...........................43

4. Atychiphobia – Fear of Failure................................57

5. Hamartophobia – Fear of Sin...................................73

6. Obediphobia – Fear of Obedience ...........................89

7. Cherophobia – Fear of Happiness...........................103

8. Euphobia – Fear of Good News .............................125

9. Xenophobia – Fear of the Unknown ......................141

10. Achievemephobia – The Fear of Success...............155

# FOREWORD

Have you ever been offended at somebody or just didn't like them the first time you met them—and then later you became great friends? That was me with Tim Hacker. (What's funny is that I have never told him this--and now he gets to read it in his book!)

The first time I met Tim was at a gathering of pastors and leaders at a retreat center in Michigan. It was time to introduce ourselves and tell what God was doing in our lives. My wife and I were in the middle of a transition from the marketplace back into vocational ministry and I was pretty stressed out. It felt kind of godly to have that kind of heaviness and anxiety on my life. It made me feel important to have problems that "big." When it was my turn to share, I made sure the group knew how significant my worries were.

Then it was Tim's turn to share. He was laughing. He was so free. He acted like he didn't have a care in the world. He had on shorts and shoes with no socks—at a pastor's meeting! Who did this guy think he was?

When the meeting broke into smaller groups, I got stuck in Tim's group. Every religious bone in my body was aching when he talked. He seemed caught up in God's goodness and talked with crazy faith about what he believed God was about to do. My faith had been reduced to just trying to find the right church to pastor and I thought God needed my help worrying to assist Him.

At the break, my wife confronted me, "Why are you acting like that towards Tim? I think he makes you nervous because he is more free than you." I didn't immediately receive her words with thanksgiving, but she was right. When I realized that Tim was carrying something that I didn't have, everything about the way I saw him changed.

Fast-forward five years. We are now great friends. He is one of the most trusted voices in my life. I call him for church advice, to bounce ideas off of him, or when I need a healthy dose of encouragement. He is a "friend that sticks closer than a brother" (Proverbs 18:24).

Tim lives what he writes about in this book. He is a person of "progressive, contagious, and incurable courage" just as his title declares. He is one of the most positive people I know and it is because he sees the world differently than most.

One of the things I love about Tim, and it is seen in this book, is that he is a great storyteller. He sucks you into his stories so that you are laughing and seeing yourself in them, all the while your mind is being renewed. He doesn't just quote scriptures at you and then tell you to "just believe!" He invites you into the story of what God is doing on the earth and helps you see how you can join Him.

This book really challenges the reader to imagine a life without fear. It sounds impossible and maybe even unwise, however, Tim reminds us that it is not God who has given us a spirit of fear and then asks, "So where does fear come from?" Tim shows how fear is a tactic of the enemy and how God has given us more than enough through Christ to win in any situation we are facing. He paints a picture of a life without timidity, caution, anxiety, worry or fear.

Through humor and personal stories as well as great revelation and insight into scripture, we are challenged to believe that God has a better way for His kids to live than in fear. One of Tim's gifts is his ability to take familiar Bible passages that we have heard taught from a certain perspective and shed fresh light on them in a way that just makes sense. He does this over and over again in this book.

I also like how he uses each chapter to address the different kinds of fears, which are common to many believers. When I saw some of the chapter titles I thought, "I don't think that I really need to read that chapter." But as I read, God dealt with me about some areas in my life where I could experience more of His "power, love and a sound mind" (2 Tim. 1:7).

Fear will rob you of God's destiny. *Gotnophobia* will stir you up and remind you of all that you have available through Christ. This is a roadmap to a life without fear.

Thank you, Tim, for field-testing this in your life and giving us this traveling guide to a life of "progressive, contagious, and incurable courage"!

Jim Baker

Senior Pastor

Zion Christian Fellowship, Powell, OH

# ACKNOWLEDGEMENTS

*Special thanks to:*

My wife Lisa – You have always believed in me even when I didn't believe in myself. Nothing good I have ever done could have happened without you by my side.

My children Joshua and Sonja – You inspire me to write for you, your children, and for your children's children.

My parents Jack and Joan – You encouraged me in the Faith from infancy. Few have the heritage you have given me.

My in-laws Roger and Shelby – You trusted me with your wonderful daughter and opened doors for my ministry.

My church family – You have heard me teach most of this book at one time or another. Your encouragement after those messages also gave me the courage to write.

My secretary Joan – You transcribed my messages and endured my "verbal processing". As a result, many of the ideas in this book found their way out of my head and onto these pages.

My editors: Cindy, Joyce, and Marlene – You covered a multitude of "writing sins".

My photographer Makahla - Your pictures made the cover look amazing.

My publishing team: Chris, Mary and Holly – With your help people are actually reading this today!

# PREFACE

Writing this book reminds me of times when I have seen a father and son on the floor putting one of those thick wooden jigsaw puzzles together. The dad knows exactly where all the pieces fit but the child is still learning. The father gives a piece to the boy and watches him study its shape and color. It's obvious to the father where it should go but the son has to think hard. He tries several spots. Finally, one works. The boy gets a little more excited with each piece that fits because the picture is beginning to be revealed.

I am that boy. I have been clumsily putting together the pieces that the Father has been giving to me. If only this book were just a twelve-piece wooden puzzle! The truth is, up till now, I have barely written anything. I feel a bit like I am a 2-year-old child trying to comprehend a 5,000-piece 3D puzzle. Yet, I also feel like my Father keeps handing me pieces. As He does He smiles saying, "Keep at it. You can do it." So, I'm not afraid to keep trying.

The good news for me is that I know that the whole puzzle is not my responsibility. I am only responsible to put together the pieces that He gives to me. I don't have to write an exhaustive book on the subject of fear. In fact, I am specifically not going to write on the topic of the fear of the Lord. There are already many good books on that subject.

My section of the puzzle is a challenging piece on the fears that hinder our lives; the fears that the enemy uses to keep us from being and doing everything that God has created us to do. My hope is that the way you think will become infected with Gotnophobia and as a result, your courage will become contagious and spread everywhere you go.

Tim Hacker

# INTRODUCTION

There are many Phobias in the world. Perhaps the most well known phobia name is, Arachnophobia (the fear of spiders) because it was also the title of a popular 1990 horror film. Another familiar phobia is Claustrophobia (the fear of closed-in places). We all know people with fear of public speaking (Glossophobia), fear of heights (Acrophobia), fear of water (Aquaphobia), fear of snakes (Ophidiophobia), and so many more.

Here (in alphabetical order) are a few that I found interesting:

Ablutophobia – *The fear of washing or bathing.* I had this as a child but my loving mother used a paddle to cure me of it.

Ballistophobia – *The fear of missiles or bullets.* I only seem to have this phobia when people are shooting at me.

Chorophobia – *The fear of dancing.* Seems to me that a lot of church people have this fear though King David did not (2 Samuel 6:14). I have heard it said by some old holiness Christians that the dancing foot and the praying knee won't be found on the same leg. (Personally, I believe the more you pray the freer you'll be to dance!)

Decidophobia – *The fear of making decisions.* I wasn't sure I should include this one but I finally made up my mind that I would.

Ecclesiophobia – *The fear of church.* This debilitating phobia is a weekly condition, which seems to strike primarily on Sunday mornings.

Eosophobia – *The fear of dawn or daylight.* This is another morning phobia that seems to be common in teenagers.

Hippopotomonstrosesquippedaliophobia – *The fear of long words.* NOW, THAT IS SCARY!

I could keep this up for a long, long time but I'll spare you. However, if you are so inclined, you can go to Phobialist.com where you'll find a list of over 500 phobias.[1]

I don't mean to be insensitive. If you do suffer from a phobia it can be very frustrating, for some even devastating. That very problem is the reason for the writing of this book. While we laugh at some of the more unusual phobias that I mentioned above, others are no laughing matter. But what if we could make every phobia a laughing matter? What if every fear could be resisted, reduced, and ultimately removed from our vocabulary and our lives? WHAT IF FEAR BECAME AFRAID OF US?

This is the simple goal of Gotnophobia. Prepare to be unafraid!

---

[1] http://phobialist.com

# Chapter 1

# Taphophobia - Fear of Being Buried Alive

*Many people die at twenty-five*
*and aren't buried until they are seventy-five. -- Benjamin Franklin*

I have been developing a phobia, Gotnophobia. It's progressive, contagious, and incurable. You probably have it too. All Christians have it though in some it seems to be in remission. That remission is temporary. It's only an attempt by dark forces to keep God's people from their real mission. God's real mission in life is an army of bold believers that will break the power of fear in the world and release the Kingdom of God to all its inhabitants.

Gotnophobia is a condition of love. We know this because the Apostle John said, "There is no fear in love" (1 John 4:18 – NKJV). The more we walk in love, the more irreversible our Gotnophobic condition becomes.

Symptoms of Gotnophobia include power, love and a sound mind. (2 Timothy 1:7) As symptoms grow stronger the patient becomes bolder. They start to think they can do anything (Philippians 4:13) and begin to manifest irrational peace (Philippians 4:7).

I have been strongly experiencing the effects of Gotnophobia since I was a boy. As a result, I have always had an overwhelming need to be with others who were also under some of the same compulsions, church people. The level of Gotnophobia I have experienced ultimately caused me to enter full-time ministry. Yep, I've got it bad. And now, perhaps for therapeutic reasons, I'm writing a book about it.

This book, and in particular this chapter, goes back to a specific outbreak of Gotnophobia I experienced one Thursday morning in 2005.


### The Skit

In the small community where I live is a group of amazing pastors. I love these guys (again, a symptom of Gotnophobia). This group has been praying together now since 1999. After prayer one morning, Tim Tracy, the pastor of Family Christian Center, showed us a skit that he called "STOP IT!" The skit was from episode 24 of season 6 of Mad TV. In this skit, a patient (played by Mo Collins) enters what looks like a typical psychiatrist's office and is greeted by the doctor, played by one of my favorite comedians, Bob Newhart.

What follows is a very funny skit in which the patient explains that she has a fear of being buried alive in a box. The doctor offers a very unexpected therapy. He tells the patient that he has two words that she needs to take and apply to her life. Then he shouts, "STOP IT!"

The Holy Spirit can and will use almost anything to inspire us. The moment Bob Newhart shouted "STOP IT" a thought came to my mind. The thought was another two words, "FEAR NOT!"

The unexpected therapy in the Mad TV skit was so surprising that it made the TV audience laugh. All of us pastors were laughing too. Indeed, surprise is one of the key elements of great comedy. Yet as I continued laughing for the remainder of the skit I found myself thinking about the words "FEAR NOT" that appear so frequently in the scripture. As I left the prayer meeting that day I knew that the Holy Spirit had spoken to me.

### Hiding In Plain Sight

It has been said that the best place to hide something is in plain sight. Could it be possible that there was a truth hidden in the lines of a secular skit written primarily to make us laugh? If we laugh at an idea will we be less likely to take it seriously?

"What truth?" you might ask. The truth hidden in plain sight is that it is possible to reject fear by choice. In the skit, the doctor's therapy was simply to tell the patient to "Stop it". We laugh because we are surprised. We are surprised because we believe that "STOP IT" is not a realistic option. Our *experience* has shown us that fear is very powerful. We all know people who have wrestled with fear and it often *seems* that more people have lost the fight than have won. You may have a fear that you've been fighting with (or more likely tolerating) for years without any real expectation of overcoming.

But what if fear isn't as strong as we have been led to believe? What if fear is actually an inferior belief system just pretending to be strong and powerful? What if fear is a **lie**?

Think about this: The number one word associated with the word "fear" in the Bible is the word "not". While you and I would think it laughable to walk up to a person who is manifesting some level of fear and simply say, "STOP IT", something very much like it happened in the Bible over and over.

One of the most widely told stories in the Bible contains an amazing scene in which a handful of shepherds are boldly told to "Fear not!" Let's look together at Luke 2:8-15 using the version quoted most often in annual Christmas pageants, the King James Version of the Bible.

> *8 And there were in the same country shepherds abiding in the field, keeping watch over their flock by night.*
>
> *9 And, lo, the angel of the Lord came upon them, and the glory of the Lord shone round about them: and they were sore afraid.*
>
> *10 And the angel said unto them, Fear not: for, behold, I bring you good tidings of great joy, which shall be to all people.*
>
> *11 For unto you is born this day in the city of David a Saviour, which is Christ the Lord.*
>
> *12 And this shall be a sign unto you; You shall find the babe wrapped in swaddling clothes, lying in a manger.*
>
> *13 And suddenly there was with the angel a multitude of the heavenly host praising God, and saying,*
>
> *14 Glory to God in the highest, and on earth peace, good will toward men.*
>
> *15 And it came to pass, as the angels were gone away from them into heaven, the shepherds said one to another, Let us now go even unto Bethlehem, and see this thing which is come to pass, which the Lord hath made known unto us.*
>
> *16 And they came with haste, and found Mary, and Joseph, and the babe lying in a manger.*

*17 And when they had seen it, they made known abroad the saying which was told them concerning this child.*

*18 And all they that heard it wondered at those things which were told them by the shepherds.*

*19 But Mary kept all these things, and pondered them in her heart.*

*20 And the shepherds returned, glorifying and praising God for all the things that they had heard and seen, as it was told unto them.*

While I have never kept watch over flocks, I have camped out overnight with friends around a fire. I can tell you that there were occasions when something a little unexpected happened. When it did, it usually spooked us pretty badly; but nothing of this magnitude ever happened to us.

Picture the shepherds sitting around, relaxing by the fire as they had done so many times before. Maybe they are having a little something to eat, their eyelids half open and half closed.

Suddenly, another world comes crashing into theirs. The light of God's glory illuminates the landscape brighter than the noonday sun. Do you think they were frozen with fear or did they scream like little girls? Nothing they had ever imagined could have prepared them for this moment!

Right in the middle of that light stood a heavenly messenger! (I'd be willing to bet that the angel God sent to announce the birth of His Son didn't look like some fair-haired child with cardboard wings and silver tinsel attached to a coat hanger floating above her head.) Any normal person would be scared spit-less. Apparently they were because their reaction caused the angel to say something. And what did he say? FEAR NOT! Basically, the angel was saying, "STOP IT!" as if he expected the shepherds to simply comply with ease. Here is the amazing thing; it appears that it worked.

15

In spite of a visitation from another realm that made them so afraid that it made their bodies hurt, (*sore* afraid – *wink*) these guys got up and boldly went in search of the Christ child. They went from fearful to bold in mere moments and quickly received the reward for their bold faith, an encounter with Jesus.

We see it over and over throughout the Scriptures. People in terrifying situations are simply told not to be afraid. Abraham, Jacob, Joseph, Moses, Joshua, Gideon, Ruth, David, Solomon, Elijah, Jehoshaphat, Hezekiah, Jeremiah, Daniel, Joseph and Mary, Zacharias, the apostles Peter, John, and Paul all had encounters directly with God, His angels or His prophets in which they were commanded not to be afraid in desperate situations. Many, many times God spoke through His prophets telling the children of Israel and Judah to not be afraid in situations where any normal person would be terrified.

When Jairus gets the worst possible news that a parent can ever hear, *"Your daughter is dead"*, Jesus calmly responds, *"Do not be afraid; only believe."* (Mark 5:35 & 36 – NKJV)

In Matthew Chapter 14 the disciples are in a boat battling a terrifying storm when Jesus shows up walking on the water. He looks like a ghost. Who can blame them for being freaked out? And what does Jesus say? "FEAR NOT!"

When Paul was on his way to Rome as a prisoner, he was on a ship that he knew would soon sink and an angel came to him saying, "FEAR NOT". Not only did Paul stop being afraid, he also boldly gave directions to everyone on the ship, saving the lives of every single person on board. (Acts 27:24)

Now, think with me for a moment. Is God in the habit of telling people to do things that He knows they are incapable of doing? That wouldn't make sense. I believe that God actually believes that we are fully able to do what He asks of us. So, when God sees the fear in us and says, "STOP IT", I believe that He actually expects us to be able to stop it!

## A Spirit of Fear

In 2 Timothy 1:7 Paul states, *"For God has not given us a Spirit of fear, but of power, and of love, and of a sound mind."* If God doesn't give the spirit of fear to us, then it's pretty easy to figure out where it does come from. I came to the conclusion a long, long time ago as a young Christian that if something wasn't from God, I didn't want it. A big part of becoming "Gotnophobic" is making the decision to reject anything that doesn't abound with the blessing of God.

We all know that every text has a context. Just in front of verse seven is another well-quoted scripture verse:

> *"Therefore I remind you to stir up the gift of God which is in you by the laying on of my hands."* (2 Timothy 1:6 – NKJV)

I have heard teachers and preachers talk about both verses six and seven but I honestly have never heard them taught in context together. (The truth is that I never taught them in context together either, though I quoted them individually in sermons for many years.) Verse six, the strong admonition to stir up the gift of the Holy Spirit that is in us, is immediately followed by another strong admonition to reject fear. Paul puts them together because he understands that the best way to overcome fear is to stay "stirred up" in the Spirit.

All throughout the scriptures we see the heroes of faith doing great exploits. More often than not, these "heroes" are initially anything but heroic. They are quite often seen manifesting some level of fear before they become transformed by the presence of God's Spirit. Then, in a moment, a greater reality takes over and they become powerful and fearless. How? It's simple. When we get on board with what God is doing, all other spirits flee. (James 4:7)

One of the keys to living a Gotnophobic life is staying aware of and stirring up the Spirit of the God that is already inside of every one of us who has experienced being "born of the Spirit".

(John 3) The NLT version of this verse says to *"fan into flames the spiritual gift"*. The idea behind this "stirring" is like taking a stick and stirring a fire that has nearly gone out. When you stir the embers they get oxygen and flame up again. As we stay "stirred up" we are then enabled to manifest the qualities that Paul is speaking of to Timothy.

### What God Has Given Us

There are three keys found in 2 Timothy 1:7 that render fear ineffective:

The first key is power. This power is transformational. We see it in the life of the Apostle Peter. Before the day of Pentecost when the Holy Spirit was given (in power) Peter was a coward. Then, after he received the Holy Spirit, he became bold as a lion. Before he received the gift he could be intimidated by a couple of servant girls. (Matthew 26:69-72) After he received the gift of the Holy Spirit, he boldly stood up and proclaimed the risen Christ before thousands. (Acts 2:14-41)

The devil is scared out of his mind that God's people are going to realize the power they have and begin to act on it. So how do we begin to access this key? It's not that hard. We repent! Repentance is simply changing the way we think. As our minds are renewed (Romans 12:2) and we begin to recognize that we have been given "the mind of Christ" (1 Corinthians 2:16) then we will realize that we are who He says we are and we can do what He says we can do.

The second key is love. The more the love of God grows in us the more Gotnophobic we become. In John's first letter we read:

> *"There is no fear in love; but perfect love casts out fear, because fear involves torment. But he who fears has not been made perfect in love."* (1 John 4:18 – NKJV)

18

The "perfect" love being spoken of in this verse is not something unattainable. The word "perfect" in western thinking is usually thought of as flawless but the word for perfect in this verse would be better understood as *mature*. The more mature our love is the more fearless we become.

As a young man, I "fell in love" with more than one girl. Because I was a Christian, when I experienced feelings for a girl, I would begin praying for her and for our relationship. I also prayed a really fearless prayer: "Lord, if this isn't the woman You want me to be with then don't let us mess up Your plan." The problem with that prayer was that He always answered it! I got dumped! *Several times.* And it always hurt. In the hurt, I would panic and try to do things to win them back, which always just made things worse emotionally for me.

When Lisa, my wife of over three decades, came along our relationship progressed very rapidly. We started seeing each other on New Year's Eve of 1977. We quickly got engaged and set September 2nd of 1978 as our wedding date. God gave us many confirmations and we were (and still are) wildly in love with each other.

About two weeks before the wedding, I was driving her back to her parents' house after a date when she said something very scary. She asked, "Are you sure we're doing the right thing?" Fear rose up in full attack mode. Was she going to dump me too? The invitations had already been sent! What would people think? We had already purchased a house and spent all our money fixing it up! I had already moved in! Was I going to be living there alone? Inside I was freaking out!!

But, there was something else going on inside of me. I loved Lisa more than I loved myself. Somehow, I saw that she just wanted to be assured that I was sure of all that God had been doing. So, I looked over at her and said, "I am completely sure. But if you aren't, we can postpone the wedding until you are ready." She just smiled and playfully said, "You're not getting out of this that easy, boy."

All of the fear melted in an instant. Her small doubt was whisked away by my reassuring words and my inner crisis was instantly devastated by her whimsical smile. Mature love casts out fear.

The third key from 2 Timothy 1:7 is a sound mind. As I already mentioned, Paul tells us in 1 Corinthians 2:16 that we have the mind of Christ. He also admonishes the Corinthians in *"taking every thought captive to the obedience of Christ"* in his second letter to them. (2 Corinthians 10:5 - NASB)

In Romans 8 Paul encourages us to set our minds on the things of the Spirit rather than the things of the flesh and then to the Philippians Paul says, *"Let this mind be in you that was also in Christ Jesus."* (Philippians 2:5 – NKJV) In Colossians we are also exhorted to set our *"mind on things above".* (Colossians 3:2 – NASB)

Paul had such a transformation in his thinking that Festus, the governor of Caesarea, said to him, *"Paul, you are out of your mind! Your great learning is driving you mad."* (Acts 26:24 - NASB) Though Paul was in chains as he made his defense before Festus and Agrippa, he was free and fearless.

### What Science Has Discovered

This idea of having a sound mind is more than a psychological state. It is also physiological. Dr. Caroline Leaf talks about it in her book, *The Gift in You*. In recent years, science has discovered that due to a phenomenon called neuroplasticity, *"The brain continues to change and grow into old age, making it an extremely unique organ both among biological and mechanical structures because it does not wear out!"*[2] She also explains, *"If the brain gets*

---

[2] Leaf, Dr. Caroline (2009). The Gift in You (p. 92). Thomas Nelson Publishers, New York, New York.

*damaged, it can change to compensate, proving that God is serious in Scripture when He tells us to renew our minds. (Romans 2:1-2) Renewing our minds is a physical reality and a scientific fact."[3] "We can alter brain anatomy in a positive love direction or a negative fear direction by how and what we choose to think."[4]* (Emphasis added)

She goes on to show that memories are actual structures in our brains. These structures are like "trees" that are either flexible healthy trees or brittle dead trees. *"You can choose whether you would like to grow a healthy "love attitude" tree that brings health and life into your brain or a toxic thorny "fear attitude" tree that will bring death into your brain."[5] "Fear is a distorted love circuit. We were created for love and all that goes with it, but we have learned to fear."[6]*

But thanks to neuroplasticity, the parts of the brain that have been damaged by fear can be repaired. Our distorted thinking can be physically altered. *"The brain releases a chemical called oxytocin, which literally melts away the negative toxic thought clusters so that the rewiring of new non-toxic circuits can happen. This chemical also flows when we trust and bond and reach out to others. Love literally wipes out fear!"[7]*

Each of these keys, power, love, and a sound mind work together to demolish strongholds of fear that are designed to rob us of the abundant life Christ came to provide for us. (John 10:10b) Through deception, our adversary the devil endeavors to make us believe he is powerful when in reality he is himself a victim of his own belief system of fear.

## Who Is the REAL Strong Man?

Satanophobia is the fear of the devil. Satan is often depicted in movies and books as a very powerful being. Many religions,

---

[3] Ibid. p. 16.

[4] Ibid. p. 22.

[5] Ibid. p. 161.

[6] Ibid. p. 149.

[7] Leaf, Dr. Caroline (2009). The Gift in You (p. 146). Thomas Nelson Publishers, New York, New York.

*including much of Christianity,* also seem to be constantly focused on the power of darkness. How is it that we even call darkness a power? Instead of talking about "the power of darkness" we should really be talking about the "weakness of darkness!"

The Apostle John makes it clear that Jesus was the light that came into the world and that the darkness did not overcome the light. (John 1:1-5) Jesus also made it clear that in Him *we* are light of the world. (Matthew 5:14) Light is never overcome by darkness. Just try to go into a room and turn on the dark! Light always pushes darkness back and darkness cannot resist the light.

How is it, then, that a defeated foe that operates in the *weakness of darkness* is perceived as being so strong? The answer is that the world is infected by a mindset that is distorted by fear. Throughout the pages of this book, we will be talking about this reality (that shouldn't be a reality at all) in an effort to change the way we think. As we renew our minds and take on the mind of Christ, we will quickly discover the lies of the enemy and begin to disable the fear Satan uses to attempt to stop God's plan for our lives.

So, what would you think if I told you that Satan and his army of lost beings are powerless spiritual creatures seeking to be empowered? What would you think if I said the devil doesn't really have any power of his own and that is why he must *"steal, kill and destroy"*? (John 10:10a) If he can get us to believe he is powerful, he can succeed in convincing us to yield to him thus giving him an illusion of "power".

A great example of this devil-empowering mindset is found in the way most Christians explain the "strong man" spoken of by Jesus in Matthew chapter 12 (also Mark 3):

> *"Or how can one enter a strong man's house and plunder his goods, unless he first binds the strong man? And then he will plunder his house."*
>
> *"When an unclean spirit goes out of a man, he goes through dry places, seeking rest, and finds none. Then he*

*says, 'I will return to my house from which I came.' And when he comes, he finds it empty, swept, and put in order. Then he goes and takes with him seven other spirits more wicked than himself, and they enter and dwell there; and the last state of that man is worse than the first."* (Matthew 12:29 & 43-45 NKJV)

In this section of scripture, a confrontation has just taken place in which the Pharisees have accused Jesus of casting out demons by the prince of demons. In the process of showing the foolishness of their argument, Jesus also explains to His disciples the workings of the demonic.

When you examine these texts together it is clear that there is a "house" full of good things that belong to a strong man. That house is being plundered. Now, let's ask ourselves, does the devil rightfully own anything good? I don't believe he does. So, if something is being plundered, it is being forcibly taken from the *rightful* owner. In Hebrews 10:34 the scripture speaks of Christians having their goods plundered during a time of persecution. From this we can clearly see that the concept of plundering in the New Testament was an activity of those working for the dark side.

Who then is the rightful owner of the house? The person that the demon is demonizing is the rightful owner of the house and in the context of Matthew 12, that *person* is called the strong man. Further examination of the words of Jesus in verses 43-45 show that the house the demon wants to inhabit is the person from which the demon was cast out. How does the demon acquire the ability to access the house? The demon *binds* up the strong man.

The devil wants us to have a mindset that makes him the strong man. Why? It's simple. If the devil is the strong man then who are we? When we see the devil as strong then we see ourselves as weak and fear keeps us from moving into the freedom Christ came to provide. However, when we see that we are the strong man then we can boldly move against the liar and stop his attempts to take what is rightfully ours.

Jesus never bound any demons. He simply cast them out. In Luke 13 Jesus sets a woman free that had been *bound* by a spirit of infirmity. It is the nature of evil spirits to bind but the nature of the Kingdom to set free.

For several decades at the end of the last century Derek Prince traveled the world teaching on demonology and ministering deliverance to thousands. One of the interesting things he taught was that calling people "demon possessed" was misleading. The word "possessed" in today's vernacular leads us to the idea that a person can be totally controlled against their will by a demonic spirit. Based on his study of the Greek language, Derek believed that it is more accurate to the original language of the scripture to say that people are demonized. I agree with him.

I believe the devil wants us to believe that he has the power to do something that God will not do. God will not take your free will from you and Satan can't! Our misunderstanding of the word translated "possessed" in most versions of the Bible has led to images in our minds where some poor soul is under the total control of a powerful devil while we nervously stand by hoping the demonic force doesn't jump on us next.

The reality is that even the most demonized person in the Bible had not completely lost his free will. Mark 5 tells us that the demoniac of Gadarenes saw Jesus from a far distance, ran to Him, and worshiped. If the demons were in complete control they would have had the man running away from Jesus, not toward Jesus.

For all of you theologians reading this, I want to encourage you to not be *afraid* to disagree with me about my position on the devil's power. Study it for yourself and come to your own conclusions but if I'm even half right, (and I believe I am or I wouldn't be writing this) then the devil is much weaker than he'd like us to believe and the fear of the devil is highly overrated! Moreover, if we have nothing to fear from the lord of fear then fear itself begins to come apart at the seams.

What if fear isn't as powerful as we fear it is? What if the enemy of our souls is doing all he can to convince us to be afraid because he's afraid of what might happen when we realize we can "STOP IT"?

We know that Satan quotes scripture. What we don't know is how much of it he really understands. I believe he does understand one thing:

> *"We can do nothing against the truth, but for the truth."* (2 Corinthians 13:8 – NKJV)

Perhaps the Mad TV skit is just an example of the devil trying to hide the truth in plain sight. Perhaps the devil is just hoping that we won't take our ability to overcome fear seriously if he can get us to laugh at the idea. And, perhaps because our enemy is unable to kill us, he is hoping to settle for the next best thing. Maybe he is just hoping to keep us from *fully* living out all the days of our lives by burying us alive in a box of fear.

You can "STOP IT!" As you read on, your thinking will be challenged and a condition I like to call Gotnophobia may begin to change your life.

# Chapter 2

# Phobophobia – Fear of Being Afraid

*The only thing we have to fear is fear itself. -- Franklin D. Roosevelt*

President Roosevelt spoke the above quote on the day of his first inauguration, March 4, 1933. The country was in a depression and fear was rampant in our nation. This quote is actually part of this larger sentence:

> *So, first of all, let me assert my firm belief that the only thing we have to fear is...fear itself — nameless, unreasoning, unjustified terror, which paralyzes needed efforts to convert retreat into advance.*

I believe that President Roosevelt understood that fear was very real. He also understood that the only thing that could truly keep our nation from breakthrough was to give in to fear. He didn't act like fear didn't exist; instead he took up the challenge to resist fear. One of the things we must do in order to overcome fear is to recognize it when it is manifesting.

Many people hate to admit that they experience fear, especially Christians. Often, if anyone suggests that we are fearful on any level, we become defensive. Yet, defensiveness is itself often a sign that fear is beginning to succeed and we indeed are becoming afraid.

What if we could become unafraid to recognize our fears? What if we became determined to recognize our fears and eliminate them? Some will argue that we cannot eliminate them. Others will argue that we shouldn't eliminate them. Some will even call their fears wisdom. I believe that we will live happier and healthier lives when we do eliminate them.


### The First Fear to Defeat

One of the first fears we need to conquer is the fear of admitting that we experience fear. Everyone experiences fear. Even Jesus experienced fear. I'm not saying Jesus was afraid. I'm saying that fear, the operating system of darkness, was manifest before Him. The scripture tells us that Jesus was *"tempted in every way, just as we are—yet He did not sin.* (Hebrews 4:15, NIV) Jesus knew what fear was but He never gave in to the temptation to participate with it.

Fear has a lot of definitions. The first one in the on-line Merriam-Webster dictionary is:

> *"An unpleasant often strong emotion caused by anticipation or awareness of danger."*

When you define fear as "awareness of danger", fear is not in and of itself a negative thing. In fact, if you can sense fear, and react to it properly, it could be considered a benefit.

## Yellow Jackets

I was in the backyard of a friend one warm summer day when I suddenly heard a buzzing noise and felt something burrowing into my hair. I instantly knew what it was. Yellow Jackets, a member of the wasp family, are common in our area. I had inadvertently stepped onto the entrance of one of their underground nests.

I was immediately aware of danger. I was also immediately moving, fast! I have only been stung a couple of times in my life but the experience has been enough to make me fully aware that I don't wish to do it again. Was I experiencing fear? By definition, yes, it was fear. The fight or flight mechanism had kicked in and I had chosen flight. I was out of danger in moments and had brushed off the little attackers without incident.

Later, when I was driving home, I wanted to make a cell phone call and suddenly realized that I had lost my Bluetooth earpiece. I immediately knew where. I drove back to my friend's house and searched the back yard. As I searched, I kept an eye out for the yellow jackets. It wasn't long before I found the Bluetooth and was back on my way.

Had I been suffering with Spheksophobia (fear of wasps), I wouldn't have been able to return to the place where I lost my Bluetooth. Fear, defined as the awareness of danger, is very different than fear that has become a phobia.

A phobia is a strong, persistent fear of situations, objects, activities or persons. The main symptom is an excessive and unreasonable desire to avoid the feared subject. Other phobia symptoms include shortness of breath, irregular heartbeat, sweating, nausea, and an overall feeling of dread. Phobias are the most common form of anxiety disorders.

You can experience fear without succumbing to a phobia. This is the very premise of the book *The Gift of Fear* written by

Gavin De Becker. Mr. De Becker is not a theologian. He is the Founder and CEO of Gavin De Becker and Associates, one of the leading private security firms in the world. I don't know Mr. De Becker's spiritual beliefs but I do know that he is very intelligent and has a great understanding about things pertaining to protecting people who may be in danger.

What most intrigued me about his book was the idea that when we feel fear, we have an opportunity to react. A correct decision can protect us while a wrong decision can devastate us. The people who work for Mr. De Becker are trained to pay attention to their feelings of fear. They are also trained to boldly take action in the face of fear in order to stop evil from being perpetrated. For these well-trained individuals, fear is never an occasion for unreasonable phobic reactions. When fear is present, determined and calculated methods of protection are quickly enforced.

My purpose for mentioning Mr. De Becker is to point out that resistance to fear is something we can and should be trained and prepared for. Many people think that fear is an uncontrollable emotion. It is not. Fear, like ALL emotions, is subject to human will. That is why King David was able to say, *"The LORD is with me; **I will not be afraid**."* (Psalm 118:6 – NIV Emphasis added) Most of us can and do control our emotions everyday.

Much of what is called "mental illness" is a lack of control over emotion. Phobias are generally only considered a mental illness at the point at which they become so out of control that the people experiencing them are unable to function normally.

Have you ever seen a child who was afraid to try something new to eat? Many of us were "that child". It's rarely a massive diagnosable phobia that keeps a child from trying a new taste. It's usually a little foolish fear that causes them to turn up their little noses to the new flavor experience that we just know they will love if they try it.

Most of us have been forced to try something new by well-meaning parents. Some of us were so stubborn that we spit it back out, even if it was good. Most of us, however, found out that our parents were right! Our fear was unfounded and we had been missing out on something really good. That is the one of the goals of fear; to keep us from something good.

## Fear of Books

In the process of writing this book I have often joked that I'm going to keep it short so that those who have a Bibliophobia will be less intimidated when attempting to read it. But seriously, how many of us actually know someone who suffers from a diagnosed fear of books?

While most of us may not know anyone who actually has Bibliophobia, I believe that almost all of us know several people who have some level of fear connected to reading. We don't think of it as a phobia because we tend to believe that phobias are overwhelming irrational levels of fear. I'm sure the number of people who are emotionally overwhelmed and run in terror at the sight of a book is a very small percentage.

We all know people who say things like, "I don't like to read" or "I'm not a very good reader". I know what I'm talking about because I was that person. I'm pretty sure that no one would have diagnosed me as being Bibliophobic and in the clinical sense I am sure that I am not. I don't feel the need to walk on the opposite side when passing a bookstore in the mall and I won't hyperventilate if someone drags me into a library. Yet for most of my life reading has been more chore than choice.

In my mid-20s a friend who worked with special needs children noticed my tendency to reverse words and numbers. He began asking me questions about my reading experience. As I talked to him about having to read sentences over and over and seeing words that looked scrambled, he told me that it was very likely that I had dyslexia.

Dyslexia is defined as a specific learning disability (or difference) that manifests primarily as a difficulty with written language, particularly with reading and spelling. Some insist it is a learning difference rather than a disability because there are so many people who are dyslexic yet are quite intelligent.

You will recognize the names: Leonardo DaVinci, Alexander Graham Bell, Walt Disney, Winston Churchill, and Albert Einstein were all people who are believed to have been dyslexic. Thomas Edison, with whom I share a birthday, was also dyslexic. Even more encouraging to me as I write this book, Agatha Christie who wrote 66 detective novels and other significant works and whose books have sold approximately 4 billion copies worldwide was also dyslexic.

While I've never had an official diagnosis of dyslexia, it makes perfect sense. During my school years I was accused by teachers of not working "up to my potential". Apparently my grades didn't match my aptitude tests. My handwriting was excellent while my spelling was atrocious.

I was driving through a small town one fall day and saw a political sign in a front yard that said "Kill Him". While I knew that small-town politics could get very heated I also knew that it was very unlikely that anyone would place such a sign in their yard. I decided to drive around the block and look at the sign again. It was indeed a political sign but this time when I read it I saw that it said "Kim Hill". She was running for office in the small town that I was in.

Over the years my determination to read has slowly improved my ability to read. While I still may not read as fast as some people, I am no longer intimidated when I need to read something.

That intimidation that I used to feel was a level of fear. Fear isn't just irrational terror. Fear is an operating system of negative belief. The intimidation I felt about reading might not have been considered debilitating, but that same intimidation hindered me on many occasions. As a student in school I would nearly freeze up every time I had to take a test that involved a time limit. I knew I could find the answers but I would try so hard to read faster that nothing I was reading made sense. As an adult, my small doubts and fears concerning my perceived lack often kept me from reading valuable books and articles simply because "it would just take me too long."

When I realized that I had a "learning difference" and that many great leaders and thinkers had overcome something similar I began to realize that I could too. I stopped being afraid of my perceived lack of reading skills and started facing the fear that was trying to hold me back. The encouragement found in their stories began to put courage in me.

Courage is not the absence of fear. Indeed, courage is never needed until fear is present! Courage is the action taken against fear that stops the evil intended by anything or anyone who is operating in fear. Today, after prayer and practicing faith to "resist the devil" I believe that I am free from the effects of dyslexia!

## Resistance Is Not Futile

We must not be afraid to admit we have battled fear. We must and should battle against fear. We must not be afraid to admit it when we are struggling with fear. With the exception of Jesus, all of us have struggled. With the exception of Jesus, all humans have succumbed to fear at some time in their lives.

Another definition for fear is to believe in something other than what God created us to believe. For some, fear becomes a lifestyle of negative belief that drives almost everything that they think or do. Fear will almost always manifest in that moment when we slip into not trusting God.

Paul Paino tells the story of traveling with Richard Roberts in Africa on a mission trip. They needed to fly from one province to another so they boarded a very rickety looking plane and began a flight that nearly scared Paul to death. Paul was sure the plane was going to crash but he could tell that Richard was not a bit worried. When they finally landed Paul asked Richard how he could stay so calm. Richard simply replied, "God told me we were to come here so I didn't doubt that He would get us here."

Fear tries to tell us something other than what God's Spirit has told us. When we are moving in fear we have taken the position of believing a lie. When we believe a lie we empower the liar.

In Mark chapter 4 we see the very familiar story of Jesus sleeping in the boat. The boat is sinking and the disciples are freaking out. (I don't blame them.) We probably all know the story. The disciples wake Jesus up and He rebukes the storm. Then He asks His disciples an amazing question.

*"Why are you so fearful? How is it that you have no faith?"* (Mark 4:40 – NKJV)

This is just another example of Jesus basically saying, "STOP IT!" when most of us would call the disciple's fear "reasonable". Jesus did not see their fear as reasonable. He had told them that they were to go to the other side. If Jesus says we're going to the other side then we can be sure we're going to the other side! When the disciples became afraid, they weren't focusing on the truth Jesus had told them. Instead, they were focusing on the lie, "We're not going to make it!"

Many stories are told of fearless martyrs. Most of them didn't give in to fear even though they knew they were going to die. How could they be so fearless? I don't doubt that in many (if not all) cases, they felt or experienced the presence of fear. They overcame because they exercised an opposite belief. When we believe God, His light comes upon us and fear retreats into the shadows.

## Choices

When we begin to understand fear as wrong belief, we can then focus and choose to believe what is right. Fear is a very strong feeling. Feelings must not direct our choices. Our choices must direct our feelings.

In the book of Daniel, we have the story of the three fearless Hebrew children, Shadrach, Meshach, and Abednego. Almost every young person who went to Sunday school has heard the story many times over. How could they be so brave? They were brave because they made a choice. Here are their words:

> Shadrach, Meshach and Abednego replied to him, "King Nebuchadnezzar, we do not need to defend ourselves before you in this matter. If we are thrown into the blazing furnace, the God we serve is able to deliver us from it, and He will deliver us from Your Majesty's hand. But even if He does not, we want you to know, Your Majesty, that we will not serve your gods or worship the image of gold you have set up." (Daniel 3:16-18; NIV)

They overcame wrong believing (fear) with right believing. When we recognize that we are struggling to believe the truth, we don't need to be afraid to admit it. We need to recognize it in order to overcome it. We can't overcome wrong belief if we can't admit to the possibility of wrong belief.

This is where many Christians fail. They instinctively recognize that it is a sin to fear; and it is. Sin at its most basic level is simply defined as missing the mark. I'll be devoting a chapter to Harmartophobia (fear of sin) later.

Since we have all sinned and fallen short of the glory of God, (Romans 3:23), perhaps a little humility is in order. When we are struggling, we need to be free to admit it to others so that we can get the encouragement we need to break through the lie and believe the truth. In fact, if we would seek assistance either from God or from other believers when fear attacks, we would often be able to "STOP IT!" before it truly becomes sin.

Most of us understand that it is not a sin to be tempted but it only becomes a sin when we give in to temptation. In the same way, it is not a sin to admit that we are being tempted with wrong belief, fear. When we admit the presence of fear we are recognizing the opportunity to take authority and respond with the proper counteraction.

### The Overdue Notice

My wife and I received a notice from the Ohio Department of Taxation telling us that we were being billed for non-remittance of our state taxes. We were not terrified, but we were *apprehensive.*

We had had an unpleasant experience years before with our taxes in which a tax preparer had failed to mail in our federal taxes and by the time we realized it, we owed a large amount extra in penalties and interest.

The first thing we did was to look through our statements to verify that the check had been cashed. At the time we had two checking accounts. One was our main checking from which we paid our regular budgeted items and the other was a special account we used to build up extra money for surprises, overages and special items that we wanted to purchase. We still use both accounts today. Lisa, my wife, keeps track of the regular checking and I'm supposed to keep track of the special checking account.

Lisa is very careful to balance her account every month. I, on the other hand, am not quite as careful. In my defense, we don't write many checks out of my account. Most months we don't write any out of the "special" account. Balancing the whole year for that account would be easier than one month in the regular account. (Did you notice how I'm becoming a little *defensive?* Could it be possible that I feel the need to defend myself out of fear that you'll think badly of me?)

Lisa keeps all of the statements in a binder so the first thing she did was to go and look for the statement. It wasn't there. The *angst* began to increase. "How could you have misplaced it?" I demanded. "We wouldn't need it if you balanced **your** checkbook!" she countered. We weren't really angry, we were just a little *tense* and *irritated*: not so much with each other but with the situation.

I got on-line and checked the account. It only took me a couple minutes to find that the check had been cashed. Good! "So it was just a mistake." I thought. Then I *worried,* "Could it have been stolen?" As I continued mulling over the situation I realized my *concern* was unlikely.

The next thing I needed to do was call the state. All of this was taking place in the early morning and I had not had my shower yet so since most government offices wouldn't be open at that time of day I decided to go finish getting ready.

While I was showering I began thinking about the call that I was going to make. How would I prove that they had cashed the check? Would I need to re-file? Should I call my CPA first? Would they want a copy of the bank statement? Since we had lost the copy the bank had sent us would we be charged for another copy? *How much was that going to cost?* **How much of my time was their mistake going to cost me? DON'T THEY KNOW THAT MY TIME IS VALUABLE?** I was getting myself pretty worked up.

On and on my mind raced. By the time I got to the actual phone call I was prepared for battle. It would have been easy to tear into the first person whose voice wasn't automated but I am glad to be able to say that I kept my *reservations* to myself. As it turned out, I ended up speaking with a very pleasant lady named

Donna who was able to correct the problem instantly. All of my *anxiety* had been a great waste of energy.

Did you notice the words in italics above? The words apprehensive, worried, angst, tense, irritated, concern, reservations, and anxiety were all used as synonyms to express some level of fear.

If you asked people in my congregation if they thought that I was at all timid, they would tell you, "NO!" People who make a living speaking publicly are usually considered to be above average in their level of confidence. But the truth is that even the bravest among us often struggle with fear.

### Fear of Weakness

One of the issues we have in facing our fears and admitting that we have them is our fear that we'll appear weak. We think that admitting fear might make us look like we don't have our act together as a Christian. We want to be just like Jesus and, because He was fearless, we feel we must be fearless too.

Indeed, Jesus is the best model for our behavior and we need to always endeavor to follow His example. Yet, while we're on our way to imitating Christ, we could start by imitating Paul. Paul invited the Corinthians to do that very thing:

> *"Imitate me, just as I also imitate Christ."* (1 Corinthians 11:1 NKJV)

Paul was a very candid leader. He went out of his way to make it clear that he was a work in progress. (Philippians 3:12,1 Timothy 1:15) He openly shared his life and wasn't afraid to admit that he experienced fear:

> *"For indeed, when we came to Macedonia, our bodies had no rest, but we were troubled on every side. Outside were conflicts, inside were fears. Nevertheless God, who comforts the downcast, comforted us."* (2 Corinthians 7:5-6 – NKJV)

38

While it is the goal of this book to help God's people overcome their fears I would never encourage anyone to be afraid to admit that they have struggles with fear. Often, leaders feel they cannot risk being vulnerable with those they lead. Paul had no such fear. He even boasted in his weaknesses:

> *"But He said to me, "My grace is sufficient for you, for my power is made perfect in weakness." Therefore I will boast all the more gladly about my weaknesses, so that Christ's power may rest on me. That is why, for Christ's sake, I delight in weaknesses, in insults, in hardships, in persecutions, in difficulties. For when I am weak, then I am strong."* (2 Corinthians 12:9-10 NIV)

As we decide to challenge our fears we will also discover that many, if not most, of our fears are the result of something being imprinted on us. Imprinting is the term psychologists use to explain how behavioral patterns are passed on to us. Many people have fears that were passed to them from others.

### Snake!

One of the places that we lived was just on the north edge of town. It was out of the city limits and felt very much like living in the country. While we only owned about one acre, most of our neighbors owned several acres each so, the houses were not at all close. As a result, we saw a lot of wildlife. Deer were very regular. A family of groundhogs visited us almost daily. Raccoon, opossum, rabbits and squirrel were all just part of the neighborhood. Oh, and don't forget snakes.

Snakes have never bothered me. I even had a few as pets when I was a kid growing up in southeastern Ohio. As a boy, I learned to identify the "safe" snakes like the garter snakes and black snakes from the "not safe" snakes like copperheads and water moccasins.

I've told a lot of people that the best way to know if a snake is poisonous is to check their eyes. The pupils in the eyes of non-poisonous snakes are round while the pupils in the eyes of poisonous snakes look like long slits or are diamond shaped. (Of course getting close enough to actually see the eyes without getting bitten is a bit tricky.)

Growing up in farm country, I learned that snakes were beneficial. Snakes eat rats. Most farmers will leave non-poisonous snakes alone and take a garden hoe to the poisonous ones.

In northwest Ohio there are lots of garter snakes and not much else. We saw a lot of snakes at our house on the north edge of town but I never needed my garden hoe. I actually liked knowing they were there because I knew that without them the field mice would be a much worse problem. (We never had a mouse in the house but we did catch a couple in traps in the garage and crawlspace.)

While the snakes didn't bother me, it wasn't quite the same for a guy in my neighborhood. He didn't like snakes, any snakes. He's not alone. I know a lot of people who have some level of Ophidiophobia (fear of snakes) and, to most of them; this fear is considered normal and reasonable. At this point, it's not my intention to argue the merits or reasonableness of Ophidiophobia. The story I want to tell you here isn't as much about my neighbor as it is about his dog. We'll call him killer. (Not his real name.)

Killer wasn't really a killer, but he sure looked like one. I don't know what his breed mixture was. I just know that he was a big, grey-brown, very protective dog. Most of the time, Killer was kept in a half-acre area surrounded by a six-foot chain link fence. He loved his family and saw everyone else as intruders. Killer had only gotten loose a couple of times but everyone in the area knew that if he was loose, it was best to keep your distance. He was exactly the kind of dog my neighbors wanted.

Killer was intended to be a watchdog and their property was definitely safe as long as he was around.

It did worry my neighbor a little that Killer might get loose and bite someone, though he never did. Shortly after we moved in, my neighbor caught me working in my backyard and gave me a very valuable piece of information. He told me the secret of being safe if Killer ever came at me. All I needed to do was say one word, *snake*. My neighbor said that if I'd say that one word, Killer would run from me. At first I thought that he was just kidding. Then he told me the story of how Killer had become afraid of the "s-word".

When Killer was a puppy, my neighbor and his wife were playing ball with Killer in the back yard. As my neighbor was reaching for the ball in the grass he suddenly realized there was a snake curled up right next to it. His wife saw the snake too and at the same moment they both shouted, "Snake!" and ran away as fast as they could toward their house. Killer ran too! He ran because they ran. The word snake scared him because his masters were scared. From that time forward, the word "snake" could make that big ferocious dog run like a scared puppy. Killer wasn't afraid of snakes but he was afraid of the *word* snake. This behavior is what psychologists call "imprinting".

One day I was in the back yard working very close to Killer's fenced in area. He didn't like it and was letting me know. After about 15 minutes of barking I walked up to within about a foot of the fence. Now he was really mad. I leaned close to his snarling face and in a voice just above a whisper I said it; "snake".

It was amazing. I don't think that poor dog could have run any harder if I would have exploded a cherry bomb in his face. He ran to the opposite side of the fenced-in area, sat down and wouldn't even look at me. Honestly, while on one hand I couldn't help but laugh, I also felt a little bad for the poor dog. It wasn't his fault. This fear wasn't his fear, it didn't belong to him, and he hadn't caused it. Yet he was under its influence.

What if I told you that no fear was your fear; no fear belongs to you, no fear is your fault? You were created in God's image and likeness. He didn't give you a spirit of fear. Fear is not part of who He created you to be.

We've all been "imprinted" with fear but that fear didn't originate with us. In reality, our fears are not our fears. They came from a source external to God and His kingdom.

As we recognize the reality that our fears aren't actually "our fears" then we won't have to be afraid to recognize those fears and deal with them. It really is much easier to say "STOP IT" to fears when we see the truth.

# Chapter 3

# Gigantasophobia – Fear of Giants

*You can discover what your enemy fears most by observing the means he uses to frighten you. -- Eric Hoffer.*

As I was listening to one of my favorite speakers talk about the story of David and Goliath a question popped in my head. Why did Goliath keep coming forward every day, day after day for forty days? Why didn't the Philistines just place him in a strategic position in their ranks and launch their attack? Surely with a guy his size in their ranks the Philistines could take the armies of Saul! Or could they?

I believe they were afraid of Saul and his armies. I believe they were afraid that they couldn't win. So they devised a plan by which they could attain their objective without actually having to fight a fair fight.

The giant, Goliath, was twice the size of any man in Saul's army. According to the scripture, Saul himself was head and shoulders above any man in Israel. Saul should have been the one to fight Goliath but apparently he, like every other man in Israel, was afraid. Saul may have thought that he was just being "reasonable" but as we discussed in chapter 2, while it is reasonable to avoid danger it is not "reasonable" to come into agreement with fear and become paralyzed.

### An Inconvenient Truth for the Devil

The truth is that the devil is afraid of us. He is afraid to fight fair and you can always be certain that Satan is trying to cheat you in everything he does. Satan's greatest fear is that we will figure out Whose we are and who we are called to be. The devil rarely attacks us directly. Instead, he most often looks for some kind of an angle, hoping that we won't catch on to his deception.

Think about this fact. The giant promised that if he were defeated the Philistines would serve the Israelites. (1 Samuel 17:9) But it wasn't true. When David defeated Goliath the Philistines all ran away, they didn't surrender. The devil is always a liar. Every temptation is an attempt to cheat us and the promise that accompanies the temptation is also a lie.

Why do we yield to temptation? We yield because we are afraid. For example, when we cheated in school when we were kids, why did we cheat? We cheated because we were afraid that we couldn't pass the test on our own. A test is not a fearful thing for the one who knows that he can pass the test. They are in fact a joy for those who know they are ready.

When I was in the 9$^{th}$ grade, I got behind in Algebra. In those days we had six grading periods in a school year. By the fourth grading period, my grade had gone down to a D on my report card. My friends Doug and Jay began to tell me that at the rate I was going I would soon be getting an F. They reasoned that in algebra, one principle builds on another. So by their calculations, I was now too far behind; I would never catch up.

I, however, knew that I was smart enough to catch up if I tried. I also knew that I really hadn't been trying. So I made a bet with them. I bet them $5.00 each (a lot of money for a kid in 1972) that I would not only improve by the next grading period, but that I would get an A. They laughed at me and said they would gladly take my money.

Then, for the first time that year, I started studying. It wasn't very long before we had a quiz. I got an A. On the next quiz I got another A. Then I got another, and another. Every time I got an A, I would hold up my paper and wave it in front of my friends. The tests became a joy to me. I actually looked forward to each and every opportunity to prove my newfound ability. I was really coming to understand what the Apostle John meant when he said, *"Count it all Joy when you fall into various tests."* (1 John 1:3) I had no fear of the tests. They had become my opportunity to prove that I could do what I said I would do. I did indeed get my "A" on my report card for that grading period. I never collected on the bet. I really didn't want the money. The personal victory was all I really needed. And, in fact, I continued to study and got an A the next grading period too.

David knew that he could pass the test. In 1 Samuel 17: 34-37 we read, *"But David said to Saul, "Your servant has been keeping his father's sheep. When a lion or a bear came and carried off a sheep from the flock, I went after it, struck it and rescued the sheep from its mouth. When it turned on me, I seized it by its hair, struck it and killed it. Your servant has killed both the lion and the bear; this uncircumcised Philistine will be like one of them, because he has defied the armies of the living God. The LORD who delivered me from the paw of the lion and the paw of the bear will deliver me from the hand of this Philistine."* (NIV) God had been with David when he overcame the lion and the bear, and he knew God would be with him against the giant. As a result, he did not respond to the giant with fear as everyone else had.

The challenge that Goliath offered was also a veiled temptation. If someone could be found to fight the giant, then the rest of the Israelite warriors would be free from any risk of harm they would experience in an all out battle. It probably seemed like a good idea at first. But as the days went by, the temptation of an easy victory became bondage. Each passing day brought more fear to the armies of God as no one came forward as their champion.

Why does the enemy tempt us? Temptation is a tool to get us off track, to keep us from our real destiny. Again, what was the temptation in Goliath's challenge? "If your man kills me we will serve you." Why is that a temptation? Can you imagine what it would be like if we had a whole nation of people come to do nothing but serve us? What would we do? Nothing! We wouldn't have to do anything. We could just goof off.

Does goofing off sound like the best method to fulfilling your destiny? Remember, work was something God gave us before the fall and before the ground was cursed. If you have nothing to do, you will have a hard time fulfilling your purpose and destiny.

Are you bored? Bored people are not fulfilling their destiny. Now, don't misunderstand. The fact that you're busy isn't proof that you're fulfilling your destiny either. But God does have something for you to do and the doing of it is designed to bring fulfillment to your life.

Temptation is always a clue to something. It wasn't Israel's destiny to live a life of leisure being served and pampered by the devil. If you are on the right track, the devil will try to derail you. Expect it!

Temptation is not an action of the devil, it is a reaction. Satan sees what we do and then reacts, and he is reacting in fear. Remember, fear is the devil's operating system.

We are like God. We are made in His image and in His likeness. We have a creative nature. Satan hates that. Satan fears that. Satan reacts to that and that's why temptation is always a reaction. What is Satan reacting to? He's reacting to what he is afraid we might do so his only hope to stop us is to distract us with temptation.

God didn't give us a conscience and give us directions to keep us from having a good time; that's the enemy's lie. God is good and He has an amazing destiny for each and every person. Fulfilling that destiny is where we find purpose and real life. Temptation and sin are Satan's tools to keep us from our real destinies.

Temptation works hand in hand with fear. Once the temptation has firmly planted itself in our thinking, a level of fear begins to work. Fear can manifest itself in several ways. We may fear missing out on some kind of experience. "Everybody else is doing it. What's the big deal? They did it and it doesn't seem to have been bad for them." This is very similar to the fear that Satan used on Eve while tempting her. He tempted her with the promise of an "experience" (wisdom) and made her afraid that God was keeping something from her.

What about you? Could there be clues to the direction you should go in the temptations you are experiencing? Isn't it just like Satan to tell you to go left when God is telling you to go right? Isn't it exactly like Satan to increase the resistance against you as you get closer to your breakthrough?

Under Saul, Israel had experienced nothing but success against the Philistines. But now, they were paralyzed with fear. A sure win had been turned into an almost certain loss.

I don't believe that they actually needed David to do what he did. If they had just attacked the enemy as they had always done they could have easily secured another victory. Yielding to the temptation to score an easy win had brought them under the power of fear.

It's the same with us. The temptation that the enemy uses against us is evidence of the enemy's fear. He knows that he cannot defeat us in a fair fight because he knows that the One who is in us is greater. (1 John 4:4) So he uses some kind of temptation to distract us. Satan knows that if he can get us off the original battle plan, he won't be as vulnerable.

If you think about it, every temptation to sin has an element of fear in it. Unforgiveness fears being hurt again. Sexual sin fears not being satisfied. Pride fears what others think. The list goes on and on.

The actions of the Philistines and Goliath were born out of fear so they passed the fear that they had to their opponents. The devil wants to give us what he's got.

While there is no benefit in fear for the believer, there is something instructive to be seen in the level of fear we experience and in the things we are afraid of.

### Your Capacity to Believe

Let's look at the story of Gideon. In the book of Judges we read:

> *"The angel of the LORD came and sat down under the oak in Ophrah that belonged to Joash the Abiezrite, where his son Gideon was threshing wheat in a winepress to keep it from the Midianites. When the angel of the LORD appeared to Gideon, he said, "The LORD is with you, mighty warrior."*
>
> *"But sir," Gideon replied, "if the LORD is with us, why has all this happened to us? Where are all His wonders that our fathers told us about when they said, 'Did not the LORD bring us up out of Egypt?' But now the LORD has abandoned us and put us into the hand of Midian."*

> *The LORD turned to him and said, "Go in the strength you have and save Israel out of Midian's hand. Am I not sending you?" "But Lord," Gideon asked, "how can I save Israel? My clan is the weakest in Manasseh, and I am the least in my family." The LORD answered, "I will be with you, and you will strike down all the Midianites together."* (Judges 6:11-16 – NIV)

Who was Gideon hiding from? He was hiding from the Midianites. And what was his destiny? It was Gideon's destiny to *"strike down all the Midianites together."*

If we can get a hold on this scripture, there is an incredibly powerful revelation here. The enemy will always work the hardest against you in the area he is the most afraid of you. Your potential in Christ is the devil's worst nightmare. Why? It's because the establishment of Christ's kingdom through you brings about the destruction of the kingdom of darkness.

The demonic realm longs to exercise a level of control over mankind. This is why a demon endeavors to return to his host when he is cast out. (Matthew 12:43) When Jesus encountered the man that had a legion of demons, the demons asked an interesting question, "Have you come here to torment us before the time?" (Matthew 8:29)

There is a time of torment for these beings that will come at the end of all things, but the very question asked by the legion of demons indicates that being "tormented before the time" was a real possibility. I believe that the demonic realm suffers every time we advance His kingdom. If you have ever been involved in the ministry of deliverance, you know that demons hate it when we worship or when we pray in the Holy Spirit. It actually seems to cause pain for many of them. When we consider these things, it isn't hard to see why our adversary seeks to limit us in the area of our greatest potential.

Are you afraid to speak in public? That's probably because you have (or will someday have) something important to say. Are you afraid to fly? Perhaps it's because you have a destiny to go places. The fear the enemy has of you is the fear he'll attempt to put on you.

Does the word "cancer" strike fear in your heart? What if the truth is that cancer is afraid of you? Could it be possible that it is God's desire to use you to pray for people with cancer and see them healed? I think it is more than just possible, I think it is very likely!

Just like Gideon, we all have more potential than our circumstances may lead us to believe. We tend to focus on our weak points. Gideon saw himself as a small man from a small clan but how did the enemy see him?

> *"Now the Midianites and Amalekites, all the people of the East, were lying in the valley as numerous as locusts; and their camels were without number, as the sand by the seashore in multitude. And when Gideon had come, there was a man telling a dream to his companion. He said, "I have had a dream: To my surprise, a loaf of barley bread tumbled into the camp of Midian; it came to a tent and struck it so that it fell and overturned, and the tent collapsed." Then his companion answered and said, "This is nothing else but the sword of Gideon the son of Joash, a man of Israel! Into his hand God has delivered Midian and the whole camp."* (Judges 7:12-14 – NKJV)

Two great armies, the Midianites and the Amalekites and a whole bunch of other people from the east had come to that place to prepare to plunder the Israelites. It would have been impossible for Gideon to count their camels, let alone the number of men. But the enemy knew something that Gideon did not know. They were more afraid of him than he was of them! The enemy knew his own destiny, and he knew the destiny of Gideon. As Gideon heard the interpretation of the dream, he realized his own destiny and fearlessly moved to fulfill it. Not only did Gideon have the capacity to believe for a miracle, but he also had a deep capacity to believe that he could do it with only 300 men.

I believe that the depth of your fear also reveals the capacity you have to believe. Remember, fear is belief in the wrong kingdom, but it is *belief*. If you have a great capacity to believe the wrong thing, you can repent (change the way you think) and use that capacity for believing the right thing. Initially, Gideon had a large capacity of belief for what he could *not* do. Then God drained Gideon's ocean of disbelief and refilled it with faith. The result was that Gideon was able to stay on task while 31,700 soldiers who could have helped went home.

Perhaps the next time you feel abandoned you need to ask yourself whether your capacity for belief might be larger than you think! Perhaps your great capacity for fear is an indicator of amazing possibilities of just how much faith you are capable of. And again, is it possible that the enemy is working to keep you terrified because your capacity to believe terrifies him? I think it is quite probable. What would we be capable of if we began to replace our greatest fears with an overflow of faith? What could stop an army of believers who were fearless?

## Fear Comes Easy to Believers

It might make sense that the greatest people of faith are sometimes also the greatest people of fear. If fear is exercising belief in the negative, then people who are able to see beyond this life, to believe in something outside the physical world, are susceptible to belief in any form. When they take their eyes off God, they are likely to believe in something, just not the right thing.

If this is true, then the greater the potential that an individual has for good through faith the greater the potential there is for evil through fear!

Consider the prophet Elijah. In 1 Kings chapter 18 he calls down fire from heaven and puts three hundred and fifty false prophets to the sword. Then we read in the very next chapter:

> *"And Ahab told Jezebel all that Elijah had done, also how he had executed all the prophets with the sword. Then Jezebel sent a messenger to Elijah, saying, "So let the gods do to me, and more also, if I do not make your life as the life of one of them by tomorrow about this time." And when he saw that, he arose and ran for his life."* (1 Kings 19:1-3 – NKJV)

How is it that a man who executes 350 men now runs from one woman? One Woman! Such great belief! His belief in God brought forth a spectacular miracle and pulled his nation back to God. His belief in one woman's threats caused him to run like a scared child.

If the enemy can get us reacting in fear instead of acting in faith, he can keep us from doing the very things we were created for. The fear that keeps us from praying for a sick friend is just evidence that something is going on in the spirit realm. The FEAR is evidence!

The presence of fear is evidence of an opportunity for faith. What would happen if believers started becoming sensitive to fear as a signal? What if we learned to respond to fear as David responded to Goliath, by running toward the situation at hand rather than running from it?

Would Satan stop using fear against us if he thought it was having a reverse effect? Perhaps. But the only way he could do that is to leave us alone and the fear that he has of us will continue to drive his attempts to limit our usefulness for the establishment of the Kingdom of God.

## The Devil Is Afraid

It was about five minutes before six in the morning when my phone rang. On the other end was a lady from our church. "Pastor, I've been up getting ready this morning and I don't know just what is going on but I think there is some kind of fear on me." Beth sounded really shaken. As I talked with her she told me that she was so full of fear that she couldn't get off the floor!

Later that day, a group of us were going to go to a healing conference and Beth was one of those scheduled to go. Earlier in the week, her job situation almost stopped her from being able to go but after prayer, things were finally worked out with her supervisor and she planned on driving up to Grand Rapids, Michigan, for the conference with my wife, Lisa.

When she called me it was her intention to tell me she wasn't going to be able to go which would then allow Lisa time to make alternate plans. But as we talked, I was able to encourage her to not let the devil keep her from going.

I reminded her "God has not given us a spirit of fear" and had her repeat it. I then said, "If God hasn't given you a spirit of fear then it must have come from the other guy. Beth, the devil must be afraid of what you'll experience at this conference because he has been fighting you all the way."

Then I heard myself admonish her, "God can't give you any fear because He doesn't have any to give but the devil is trying to give you his fear because that's all he's got. The fear that you're feeling is the fear that he's feeling because he is terrified about what might happen to you this weekend."

The fear began to lift off of Beth and, after we prayed, she wrote down 2 Timothy 1:7 and took it to work with her. For the rest of the morning she repeated it over and over. That afternoon she drove up to the conference with Lisa.

When she got to the conference the fear tried to come on her again. This time several people gathered around her and ministered to her. The fear was finally completely broken.

The Sunday morning following the conference Beth testified to the church about her experience and told how she was set free. Following her testimony, we prayed with about a dozen more people who were battling with some type of fear. Just as Beth had been set free, others were now breaking the power of fear. No wonder the devil was so afraid of seeing Beth go to that conference!

It's impossible to give someone something you haven't got. God can't give us fear because He hasn't got any to give but the devil is the most fearful being in existence. While love is the operating system of the Kingdom of God, fear is the operating system of the prince of this age. Could it be possible that the devil torments us with the very terror that he himself is experiencing? I believe that it is exactly what is happening.

The fear the devil has of you is the fear the devil will put on you. Satan wants you to carry his fear for him.

When the Magi told Herod about their mission, he instantly became fearful. He was afraid of the possible rise of another king so he murdered all of the children in Bethlehem, terrorizing the whole region. What is true of evil leaders is true of the evil spirits inspiring them.

The demons in the demoniac of the Gaderenes fearfully questioned, "Are you here to torment us before the time?" (Matthew 8:28) James tells us that the demons believe in Christ and they tremble. (James 2:19) It is vitally important that we begin to recognize the power of Christ in us. As we do, we will terrorize dark spirits and see the captives set free!

So, what is the conclusion? Temptation and fear are co-operating in the operating system of the enemy. When we begin experiencing them, we need to turn the tables on the enemy, recognize who is behind them, and begin to look to see what the enemy is trying to steer us away from.

Is there a giant of fear in your life? Is he offering some sort of temptation to you in an effort to keep you from your great destiny in Christ? Is he trying to get you to focus on all that might go wrong rather than all that is going right? When you see fear for what it is and what it's up to you will have the power to "STOP IT!

# Chapter 4

# Atychiphobia – Fear of Failure

*I failed my way to success. -- Thomas Edison*

In high school, I watched my older brother Jeff attempt to wear contact lenses. In those days, because of astigmatism, his only alternative was to use hard lenses. As many of you know, those types of lenses weren't very comfortable. But comfort really wasn't his biggest problem. Once he got them in, he didn't seem to have a lot of trouble with them.

His biggest problem was just simply getting them in. I watched him insert them several times. He would lay a six-inch wide mirror flat on his dresser. Then he would look down into the mirror as he slowly brought the contact lens up to his eye on one finger to put it in place. His eyes were VERY sensitive. Just thinking about touching his eye made his eyes water. The process always required several tries for each eye and rarely took less than 30 minutes. During the procedure, tears would fall onto the surface of the mirror. The mirror had a one-quarter inch lip all around its outer edge and by the time Jeff got finished, that mirror would be nearly overflowing with tears. Jeff really wanted to ditch his glasses but he found the contacts just too much hassle.

I remember watching my brother's valiant effort thinking, "I could NEVER do that." My eyes too had always been sensitive. Just watching Jeff try to put his contact lenses in gave me the willies. I couldn't touch my eyes and just thinking about it made me tear up.

When I married Lisa, she had already been wearing hard contact lenses for a few years. I marveled as she just popped her contacts in easily everyday. I told her many times that I was sure I could *never* wear contact lenses. The good news was that I had great vision so it wasn't an issue.

Fast-forward about 30 years. I'm wearing glasses because I need them to read. I'm a pastor so of course I speak in front of people regularly. At first I tried reading glasses but I found myself taking them off to look at my audience and then putting them back on to read. For me, that just seemed too much like work. Then I tried sliding them down my nose and looking over them. Yuck! It just felt so unnatural for me.

Next, I went to bi-focal glasses. It worked okay for teaching and preaching but I also do some worship leading. The microphone is stationary so it was my eyes that needed to move up and down the pages of music. As many of you reading this know, with bi-focal lenses, people unconsciously move their heads slightly to see out of the lower part of the lenses. My head movement was causing my mouth to move away from my microphone. When I would try not to move I would not see clearly resulting in wrong chords, words or even worse, just plain getting lost. I found myself getting frustrated. Then I had the idea, "Contact lenses would be really great!" Then just as quickly I remembered, "I could NEVER wear contacts."

In my younger years I would not have seen the idea of being unable to wear contacts as a fear. To me, it was just a reality of the physiological make up of my eyes. My thought process was that some people can touch their eyes and some people simply can't. In the last few years, however, I had come to realize that there are many things we *think* we can't do. When the "I could NEVER" thought came up, something inside me rose up and rebelled against it.

I decided I would get contact lenses. Of course the next thought I had was, "But what if I can't get them in? What if I find out that I can't wear them comfortably?" Fear of failure keeps a lot of people from even attempting something they aren't sure about. Couple that kind of thinking with a poverty spirit ("If I don't wear them it will waste money") and giving up can masquerade as just good old common sense.

I recognized the challenge and made an eye appointment. I KNEW I could do it. Failure was not an option. Within a couple weeks I had gotten the contact lenses and the very first time I tried I got them in easily. The apprehension was a lie and the truth had set me free!

Now, I realize that this "fear" was a small thing. There have been several small things that I have overcome in just the last few years but I won't bore you with my list. I will tell you something that you have probably heard before; what you tolerate will dominate. If you tolerate failure it can start a momentum of failure. I will also remind you of Solomon's words:

> *"Catch us the foxes, the little foxes that spoil the vines"* (Song of Solomon 2:15a – NKJV)

Little fears, like little foxes, can gnaw away at our courage and limit our fruitfulness before it can get started. Fear of failure will often stop us before we even begin.

### Fear of Failure Is a Thief

At this point I want to mention something that happened in conjunction with my victory over my fear of failure connected with my contact lens story. Not only did I successfully start wearing contact lenses, but I also made some money that the fear of failure would have cheated me out of!

About one month after starting to wear contact lenses, my first pair started to get itchy and uncomfortable. I had been told it would happen by my eye doctor. She explained that soft contact lenses build up with proteins that can't be cleaned off and so the lenses have to be thrown away and new ones put in. When it came time to throw my first set away a question popped into my mind. Why can't the protein be cleaned off? Aren't the lenses made of plastic? Isn't there some way of cleaning the protein off without harming the soft material they are made from?

I began to research. I found out that the microscopic protein buildup could be safely removed and developed a device to do it. I wanted to call the product "Revitalens" and immediately went on line and purchased the domain name revitalens.com. After several months of working on my idea I was walking through a drug store and saw the name "Revitalens" on a bottle of contact solution. "Oh dang!" I thought. "Now I won't be able to use that name." But then I had another thought! "I own the rights to the domain name! I wonder how much they would pay to have it?"

I contacted the company who made Revitalens and they paid me nearly 200 times the amount I had invested into the domain name. It didn't make me rich, (the amount was $4,000.00) but it sure didn't hurt! Then I simply thought of another name for my device. I don't yet know if the device will ever make money but I do know that the devil definitely did not want me to get contact lenses. My fear of failure was a ruse to keep me from more than just being able to wear contact lenses.

## What If We Are Already More Successful Than We Think?

Most of us have been in situations where we prayed for something or someone but haven't seen any results. Let me repeat that last line but this time I want to add emphasis. I said, "Most of us have been in situations where we prayed for something or someone but haven't *seen* any results." Is it that our prayers aren't getting results or is it that we aren't *seeing* the results? The difference is subtle but profound. Why? Because the writer of Hebrews says, "faith is the substance of things not yet **SEEN**". There are times when the fear of failure can make us focus on what we are NOT seeing and miss what we could be seeing. What if we are already more successful than we think?

In Luke 1:37 the angel tells Mary that nothing is impossible with God. The Greek word for nothing is a compound word that translates literally *"not any word"*. The Greek word for "word" is *"rhema"* which is a present God-breathed word. The idea that we normally take from this phrase is that God can do anything, and that is true, God can do anything. Jesus says as much in Matthew 19:26 – *"Jesus looked at them and said, "With man this is impossible, but with God all things are possible."* (NIV) But the verse in Luke is a different wording and could be translated, "This present spoken word cannot be without power with God".

So, as I was thinking about this, the thought came to me that *"nothing"* is an "impossibility" with God. God is not a being Whose nature is to do nothing. He is a God of action and creativity. It is against His nature to do nothing when there is something that needs done. It is against His nature to not respond to the prayers of His people, especially when they ask in the name of His son. Jesus also said, *"And I will do whatever you ask in my name, so that the Son may bring glory to the Father.* (John 14:13, NIV)

When we pray, it sometimes seems like nothing happens. But now I am beginning to believe that having nothing happen is not possible. If we pray to a God whose nature refuses to do nothing, then He must be doing something. There are several examples in the Bible of times when God was up to something and men couldn't or wouldn't see it.

Naaman, the Syrian, nearly missed his healing because the prophet gave him directions that were sent by God but were not what Naaman expected. (2 Kings 5) Jacob failed to recognize that God's presence was in the place where he was sleeping. (Genesis 28) Ananias attempted to talk the Holy Spirit out of going to bring healing to the Apostle Paul. (Acts 9) Almost every great leader had moments where he failed to clearly see what God was up to.

Could it be possible that in looking for a desired result we fail to see important steps that need to be taken first? What if every time we prayed, we believed that something did happen because "nothing" is not an option with God? If God is indeed doing something, and we learn to see it, then instead of having our faith falter because nothing seems to be happening, perhaps our faith would begin to rise as we see what He *is* doing.

### God Is with You

Ask yourself, "Is God with me? Is there ever a time when God is not with me?" What did He say? *"I will never leave you or forsake you."* (Hebrews 13:5) There is NEVER a time when His presence is not with you. Many of you can check it by using your prayer language. Is your prayer language still there? Of course it is! His Holy Spirit is constantly with us, even when we sin. (I'll say more about fear and its relationship to sin in chapter 5.)

So, you and God are going down the street and you see someone with a need. If you pray for them, is God going to cease being with you? Never! He cannot stop being with you. He cannot fail to keep His promise. So if you decide to pray for the needy, does He leave? Again, He cannot. He has bound Himself by His promise. He must stay with you.

Now if God is with me when I pray, and "nothing" is impossible *with* God, then something has to happen when I pray. When we begin to believe, really believe that something is going to happen when we pray, we have a greater motivation to pray.

"But I have prayed and nothing has happened." That cannot be true unless God was not with you. Something did happen. The question is not, "Did something happen?" The question is, "What happened?" God always does something in response to the prayer of someone He is with, ALWAYS! Something is always sent but too often what is sent is not quickly received.

## Something WAS Happening!

Take again the example of Naaman, the Syrian. (2 Kings 5) He did not get the kind of reception he was expecting. His obedience was only rewarded after the seventh time that he dipped himself in the river. Did nothing happen the first six times? Some have said as much but I don't believe it. I believe each time he dipped *something* happened. I believe that the first six dips cleansed something on the inside before the seventh cleansed the leprosy on the outside.

In his book *The Hidden Power of Prayer and Fasting*, Mahesh Chavda tells the story of praying for a blind woman in Haiti. Each night during the meeting her granddaughter would lead the blind woman to the front for prayer. Each time Mahesh prayed, the blind woman would be knocked to the ground by the power of God but when she got up, she was still unable to see. It seemed as though nothing was happening yet Mahesh knew by the anointing he felt that something *was* happening.

By the fourth night it was beginning to become a little discouraging. Mahesh prayed, the woman fell, the blindness remained and Mahesh could only tell her to come back "tomorrow night". The amazing thing is that the woman did come back. She came back every night for the entire week!

On the last night of the series of meetings, Mahesh prayed again. The blind woman fell down under the power again but this time she got up fully healed. It was wonderful, but Mahesh couldn't help wonder why it hadn't happened on the first night of the meetings. Months later God gave him a vision. I'll let Mahesh tell the rest of the story.

> *I had wondered many times about the seven days I had prayed for that blind woman, and suddenly I found myself reliving those times in living color. Only this time I knew I was seeing through the eyes of the spirit. As this woman came up for prayer in each service, the Lord showed me that there was a creature that looks similar to an octopus with several tentacles wrapped around the woman's eyes. Every time I prayed, the anointing of God would hit her and knock off one of the tentacles.*

> *During the second prayer, a second tentacle was supernaturally removed. During the third prayer, a third tentacle came off. Finally, on the last night in the last service, the woman came forward with a single tentacle still wrapped around her eyes. It was like a spirit of blindness, the main demon that had kept her bound in a world of darkness. When I prayed for her the last day, the last tentacle came off and she could see clearly.*

> *The Lord revealed to me that at times, demonic*

*obstructions hold us or cling to us with several arms.
Every time you pray under the anointing, something
happens. You can count on that.[8]*

Every time Mahesh prayed, something happened. What if it
is true of all of God's children? What if we are all getting more
results than we realize but just aren't *seeing* it?

## Eyes to See

When Elisha's servant could not see the armies of God, that
didn't mean that they weren't there. Elisha could see what his
servant could not see:

> *"When the servant of the man of God got up and
> went out early the next morning, an army with horses and
> chariots had surrounded the city. "Oh, my lord, what
> shall we do?" the servant asked. "Don't be afraid," the
> prophet answered. "Those who are with us are more than
> those who are with them." And Elisha prayed, "O
> LORD, open his eyes so he may see." Then the LORD
> opened the servant's eyes, and he looked and saw the hills
> full of horses and chariots of fire all around Elisha."* (2
> Kings 6:15-17 – NIV)

Notice that before Elisha prayed for his servant's eyes to be
opened, he commanded his servant not to be afraid. Fear was
keeping Elijah's servant from seeing what God was doing. When
fear was dealt with, then a prayer for revelation could be prayed
and the servant could see what could not be seen.

I now believe that something has to happen every time that I
pray. Why do I believe this? I believe it because He is with me
and *"nothing is impossible with God".* Do the people that I pray for
always get the complete instantaneous breakthrough they need?

---

[8] Chavda, Mahesh (1998) The Hidden Power of Prayer and Fasting (p.
48-49) Destiny Image Publishers, Shippensburg, Pennsylvania.

Not yet, but many do and more get a breakthrough than when I don't pray! Moreover, everyone I pray for gets **something** because "nothing" is not an option. Instead of focusing on what didn't happen (yet), I am now looking to see what did happen. SOMETHING ALWAYS HAPPENS!

### Measuring Success

Doctors and hospitals are paid huge amounts of money to make "improvements" in their patient's quality of life. Even small measures of success are considered valuable and are appreciated. In a similar manner, almost every time I have prayed for someone they have felt somewhat better, if not physically, at least mentally. Just the idea that someone cared enough to take time to pray will lift their spirits. Most of the time when I have prayed the prayer of faith, they feel some physical improvement. Often within a few days, they will completely recover and, of course, many have been instantly healed.

We need to begin to realize that our prayers are effective. Failure is not an option because we *know* that *something* is going to happen. As something begins to happen, we need to ask Holy Spirit for eyes to see so we can co-operate with what God *is* doing. As we pray more often and see into the Spirit more effectively, we will increase in our ability to help those who need miracles receive them.

Imagine trying to be good at something you rarely do. I try it every year with golf and I can testify that it just doesn't work. Most of the time I hit just enough good shots in nine holes to keep me hanging on to the clubs for one more year. I realize that I will never be great at golf because I don't devote enough practice to it.

Most Christians have the same problem with miracle working prayer. We've taken enough "shots" at it to know what it is to experience something amazing but we have also had those times that we just didn't "connect". We must keep swinging. We must not quit. God's call on us to "do the works" that He did is not just a game. (John 14:12) He doesn't want us to leave it up to a few "pros". It is His kingdom purpose to see every believer begin to really believe. When they do, the fear of failure will disappear and signs, wonders and miracles will become part of the normal Christian life.

## More than Facts

Luke tells this story:

> "When He (Jesus) had stopped speaking, He said to Simon, "Launch out into the deep and let down your nets for a catch." But Simon answered and said to Him, "Master, we have toiled all night and caught nothing; nevertheless at Your word I will let down the net." And when they had done this, they caught a great number of fish, and their net was breaking." (Luke 5:4-6 – NKJV)

If you read the full story you will see that Peter and his men were washing their nets after a full night of fishing. I'm sure they were ready for some sleep. I know I would be. Jesus had already kept them from being able to go straight to bed by asking to use their boat for a place to teach from. Now He was asking them to get the nets that they had already cleaned and put away and take them back out and mess them up.

Peter fished for a living. He knew his business. He knew the facts. What Jesus was asking him to do made no sense. He was tired and to let the nets down now would mean a lot of work for no reward. But Peter said, "Nevertheless".

A "nevertheless" decision is a decision to not pay attention to the facts of the situation but rather to act in spite of the facts. Peter said to Jesus, "Nevertheless at Your word I will let down the nets" and as a result he received a miracle. If he had done less he would have received less but, his decision was NEVER-the less and, as a result, he did not receive the less but instead he received the MORE!

David Crone, the senior leader of a church called The Mission in Vacaville, California, tells a story about his daughter. She wasn't able to get pregnant and longed to have a child. She had been prayed for dozens (maybe hundreds) of times but she wasn't able to conceive. She and her husband then decided to adopt. Life was good. They already had an adopted child when a guest speaker came to their church to minister. The speaker said that he felt led to pray for women who had not been able to have children. David wondered if his daughter would even come forward. At first she didn't. Then, there she was. Once again she was stepping forward to be prayed for. A short time later she conceived.

Isn't it amazing that we stop praying for things after a while even though we say we believe that prayer could help? Why do we do that? Could it be the fear of failure? Think about it this way, if you suffer from chronic pain and one day someone comes along with a possible medical breakthrough that wouldn't hurt you but could help, would you try it? Of course! What if they told you that you might need to try it several times before it worked? What if they said that on the average, it worked once for every one hundred times it was attempted? Would you keep trying? I know I would.

So, why is it that we try prayer a couple of times and then give up? For every disease or need known to man there are testimonies of people who have seen prayer make a difference. God is no respecter of persons. If He did it for others, He will do it for you!

Now, I just asked the question, "Why is it that we try prayer a couple of times and then give up?" The first time I asked it rhetorically but, by now you know that whatever reason we give for not getting prayer, it is almost always a cover for the fact that we are wrestling with some type of fear.

## Ears to REALLY Hear

In 1980 I was traveling with a band called Judah. We hadn't yet seen God do any tremendous miracles with our ministry but we believed He could. In one meeting in West Virginia, Sam, one of the members of our team, preached a word on having "ears to hear". Though he had meant this metaphorically, when the altar call was given, eight people came forward seeking prayer for some level of physical hearing loss. What else could we do? The fish were already in the boat. There was no throwing them back. So, we prayed and all eight were healed. From that time on, healing became a big part of our ministry.

Later, we were asked to do special music for a meeting in Pennsylvania. As I sat listening to the pastor of the church speak about the power of the body of Christ to bring healing, the Lord gave me a very specific word about a young man in a wheelchair in the back of the room. The Lord told me that his name was John and that I was to have the congregation stretch out their hands as I called out John's name and told him to get up and walk.

Needless to say, I was scared to death. What if I was wrong about his name? What if he didn't get healed? I immediately began co-operating with the operating system of fear. My mind was racing instead of resting. When it came time for our band to play a closing song, I awkwardly pulled the pastor aside and nervously blurted out, "I want to pray for the guy in the wheelchair!" He looked at me and said that I could do so following the service, "not now".

I knew that if I didn't do it the way the Lord had told me to do it that the result wouldn't be as good but I didn't want to offend the pastor and I was, after all, in submission to his authority.

Immediately following the service I went to see the young man in the wheelchair. His name *was* John. Needless to say I was devastated. I prayed with him anyway but I didn't see any breakthrough.

I then went to the pastor. "Why didn't you let me pray?" I asked. "God had even given me his name." "You didn't tell me that!" he responded. He then told me of all the times John had been prayed for and named a list of famous people who had prayed for him. If I had taken the time to explain what was happening, he would have *wanted* me to pray. But he also added that he didn't want the hopes of the people of the church to be dashed if I missed God.

I am not telling this story to assess blame. I also am not trying to build any theology based on this experience. What I want to do is point out that fear was able to keep us from seeing God do something.

Years later I met the successor of that church and told him the story. He remembered John and told me that he had passed away. John never got out of that wheelchair. While I don't carry any condemnation over what fear kept me from doing that night, I do keep the memory of it as a reminder of just how foolish fear can make us.

I have heard several speakers tell the story of Heidi Baker who prayed for over 100 people who had some level of hearing loss before she saw the first one healed. She didn't give up because she had received a prophetic word that she would see deaf ears opened. While I can't say exactly what happened to the first 100 she prayed for, I believe something happened to each one of them. More than that, I believe that something was happening to Heidi each time she prayed. While we might think that she would become more discouraged with each apparent failure, I believe that it was just the opposite. Every time she prayed, God did something in her as well.

Now, in every village in Mozambique in which she ministers, she asks the people to bring her all the deaf and she boldly says that they will all hear, and they DO! Now she sees thousands healed of hearing loss and other diseases.

Jesus said, *"If you have faith as small as a mustard seed … nothing will be impossible for you."* (Matthew 17:20, NIV) When we fully overcome the fear of failure, nothing will be impossible because we will always do something. When it comes to the fear of failure, we can "STOP IT" by asking the Holy Spirit what to do and then just simply doing it.

# Chapter 5

# Hamartophobia – Fear of Sin

*If one by one we counted people out for the least sin, it wouldn't take us long to get so we had no one left to live with. For to be social is to be forgiving. -- Robert Frost*

There is the fear of sin and there is the sin of fear.

The fear of sin was the sickness of the Pharisee. The Pharisees were afraid of people who had sin in their life. They were afraid that they might be contaminated. This fear is why they could not touch the lepers. While the Pharisees dared not touch the lepers because they feared becoming unclean, Jesus had no such fear, so he touched the lepers and they became clean.

Their fear of sin caused them to commit the sin of fear. It is still a popular sin among people today, even among those that say they are people of faith. It is sin to fear. Fear is the operating system of the enemy. Love is the operating system of the Spirit. When we fear we co-operate with the enemy and inadvertently assist him in establishing his kingdom.

The Pharisees called their sin piety. They even blamed it on the fear of the Lord. But it was not fear of the Lord. It was a fear that was based in pride. Pride fears that somehow God is not who He says He is. Pride says that somehow God might be holding out on us. Pride is afraid to place trust in anyone but self.

### Missing the Mark

Sin in the original language can be translated "missing the mark". Using this understanding we see that when we sin we fail to hit the target. One of the big problems with fear-based thinking is that it tends to focus on the miss. We focus on how far from the target the miss was. Then we gauge the severity of the sin using a "further from the target the worse the sin" mentality. As we primarily focus on the sin, we continue to miss the mark which, by definition, would be living in sin.

When we sin, we need to be careful that we don't forget there was a mark we missed. If sin is missing the mark then there is a positive alternative that would be "hitting the mark". The way to stop missing would not be found by focusing on how badly we have missed but rather by focusing on how to correctly hit the target. Let's try a few examples:

Do we believe that it is a sin to eat? Of course not! We do, however, know that it is a sin to overeat. Yet, we don't consider overeating as bad a sin as some other overindulgence. Is the real problem overeating or is it improper eating? We all have to eat. It's unavoidable. It is right to feed the need. It's just wrong (a sin) to feed the need improperly.

Cravings aren't the problem. Satisfying those cravings isn't wrong. Satisfying those cravings in the wrong way is the problem. Nutritionists will tell you that when you eat the wrong things to satisfy cravings, it will seem to satisfy for a moment but will result in making the cravings worse in the long run. Beating yourself up for eating the wrong thing and making up your mind that you won't "do that again" will not make the cravings go away.

So what should you do? Find the right thing to eat! Hitting the mark is the solution. Let's look at another area:

Sex is good, right? We all have a sex drive; it was given to us by God. That means God *wants* us to have sex. God has also created a context in which sex is a beautiful thing. It's called marriage. Marriage is a covenant between a man and a woman in which a spiritual, emotional, and physiological union is created.

God's version of marriage is the version that produces *life* in all three areas of our beings: body, soul and spirit. We also know that for every version there is a perversion. God isn't against something less than the real version because it offends Him. God is against the per-version because it offends those who are trapped by it. The perversion can only provide an experience that is less than God's best. God loves us so He naturally wants the best for all of us.

Any time sex takes place outside of the context of God's

plan for our lives it misses the mark; it is sin. But just as sex in the wrong context can miss the mark, sometimes, not having sex is a sin. Consider the following passage:

> *"Now concerning the things of which you wrote to me:*
>
> *It is good for a man not to touch a woman. Nevertheless, because of sexual immorality, let each man have his own wife, and let each woman have her own husband. Let the husband render to his wife the affection due her, and likewise also the wife to her husband. The wife does not have authority over her own body, but the husband does. And likewise the husband does not have authority over his own body, but the wife does. **Do not deprive one another** except with consent for a time, that you may give yourselves to fasting and prayer; and come together again so that Satan does not tempt you because of your lack of self-control."* (1 Corinthians 7:1-6 NJKV, emphasis added)

The loving God who created us is not keeping anything good from us. God doesn't keep things from us; He keeps things for us. He understands our needs and He wants to see them *fully* fulfilled.

The problem with sin is not as much about what we are *attracted to* when we sin but rather what we are *distracted from*. Every sin is intended to lead us away from the better thing that God intended for us.

Sin is always second best. When we sin we are actually settling for less than God meant for us. Temptation should set off an alarm. When we are tempted we should be thinking, "Hey, what blessing is the devil afraid I'm about to get?"

After we have missed the mark, instead of being devastated about what we did, what if we became more aware of greater good that we missed? If we stop focusing on our failure and begin to search for the underlying motive of the enemy, then we might find the motivation to help us avoid the robbery we just experienced the next time the devil attempts to cheat us. If our view of sin was less like "look what you did" and more "look what you could have had" then we would be much more effective in helping others and ourselves.

## The World Needs Our Help

How are we as the church responding to the needs of the world? Is our focus on pointing out where people have missed the mark or showing them how to hit the mark?

The best way to meet the need is to beat the need. Stay ahead. Be ready. We know certain needs are going to present themselves. When we focus on our failures we aren't preparing for success but rather waiting in dread (fear) for the next failure.

We have a warped view of sin. Since the basic Greek word for sin comes from the idea of missing the mark, and we all miss the mark, then anything less than the center of the center of the center is less than perfect. So, the reality is, most of the time we will be contending with less than perfect results.

Life is messy. Fear never makes a mess better. When we come upon a mess, the simple thing to do is clean it up, not freak out. Sin is not as much about people doing evil as evil doing people.

Sin is not powerful. Sin lost its power when Jesus established the new covenant. 1 Corinthians 15:56 tells us that the power of sin is the law. So since Jesus satisfied the requirements of the law by His sacrifice, we are no longer under the law but under grace.

When we see sin, we need not fear it, we need to clear it. We haven't been called to condemn sin. That has already been done. We have been called to clean it up and cancel its effects. Sinners are victims of sin.

People who know how to clean aren't afraid of getting dirty. Jesus said, *"Make the inside of the cup clean and the outside will be clean also."* (Matthew 23:26 – NKJV) Being afraid to get among the sinners for fear it will rub off is like being afraid to clean up a mess because you might get dirty. Our clean hearts will keep us safe from a smudge here or there as we work to wipe out sin.

Our attitude needs to be, "Hey. Its just sin." Clean it up and move on. Don't stand around lamenting it. That's just stupid.

### The Bicycle

When I turned 11 years old, along with my other birthday gifts, my dad promised to buy me a new bicycle. Even though my birthday came in February, my dad said he would wait until school was out in June to get me the new bike.

With the promise in mind, we began shopping for the new bike. I remember being at the Sears store and having my dad show me a 36-inch 10-speed touring bicycle. He told me that it was the bike that I should get.

But across the aisle was another group of bicycles, and they were so cool. I saw the one I wanted. It was a golden Schwinn 24 inch bicycle with high-rise handlebars and a tiger print banana seat. It was one of those bikes that were really easy to "pop wheelies" on. It had a 5-speed stick shifter right in front of the seat. Oh baby! That was the bike for me.

But my dad kept telling me to look again at the bigger bike. He kept trying to tell me that as I got bigger I wouldn't want the smaller bicycle. I didn't listen. The more he tried to tell me about the other bicycles the more determined I was to get the "cool" bike.

Finally, school was out. I made my choice. I got what I wanted. It was amazing. All of my friends thought it was the coolest bicycle ever. I had an awesome summer. Yep, it was ONE awesome summer.

As all adults know, time moves so very quickly. Before I knew what had happened it was the next summer. I was taller and the bike felt smaller. Worse than that, my bike was going out of style. It was no longer as cool as it used to be.

Then several of my friends' dads bought them new bikes. You guessed it; they all got 10-speed touring bikes. Not only was my bike too small and no longer in style, but no matter how hard I pedaled, there was no way I could keep up with the bigger bikes.

Was it a sin not to buy the bigger bicycle that my father wanted for me? After all, it was my choice. It's not like I lied or cheated or stole something. But, I did miss an opportunity to honor my father. More than that, I missed my father's greater good for me. I indeed missed the mark.

Why didn't I listen to my father? It wasn't because I wanted less than the very best. Most people don't wake up in the morning thinking, "How can I make dumb decisions today so that I end up with less than the very best?" Generally, we want the best, but we just don't know what it is or know how to get it. Was it possible that I didn't listen because I wanted to be cool in the eyes of my friends? Yes, I'm sure that played a part. At the time, I didn't recognize it as "the fear of man" but that's probably what it was. There is some type of fear associated with every sin because sin operates in the fear operating system.

Fear is often associated with the feeling that we are missing out on something. Eve's first sin was connected to the lie, *"For God knows that when you eat of it your eyes will be opened, and you will be like God, knowing good and evil."* (Genesis 3:5 NIV) The insinuation of the serpent was that God was holding out on Adam and Eve.

The real truth is that a loving father wants to give everything that he has to his children. *"He who did not spare His own Son, but delivered Him up for us all, how shall He not with Him also freely give us* ***all things?"*** (Romans 8:32 – NKJV, emphasis added)

### The Fear/Sin Connection

In the Book of Nehemiah, there were some people who were trying to get Nehemiah to cooperate with the operating system of fear. They had been writing to him in an effort to discourage him in what God had called him to do. Let's pick up the story in verse 5 of chapter 6:

> *"Then Sanballat sent his servant to me as before, the fifth time, with an open letter in his hand. In it was written: It is reported among the nations, and Geshem says, that you and the Jews plan to rebel; therefore, according to these rumors, you are rebuilding the wall, that you may be their king. And you have also appointed prophets to proclaim concerning you at Jerusalem, saying, "There is a king in Judah!" Now these matters will be reported to the king. So come, therefore, and let us consult*

*together.*

> *Then I sent to him, saying, "No such things as you say are being done, but you invent them in your own heart." For they all were trying to make us afraid, saying, "Their hands will be weakened in the work, and it will not be done." Now therefore, O God, strengthen my hands.*

> *Afterward I came to the house of Shemaiah the son of Delaiah, the son of Mehetabel, who was a secret informer; and he said, "Let us meet together in the house of God, within the temple, and let us close the doors of the temple, for they are coming to kill you; indeed, at night they will come to kill you. "And I said, "Should such a man as I flee? And who is there such as I who would go into the temple to save his life? I will not go in!" Then I perceived that God had not sent him at all, but that he pronounced this prophecy against me because Tobiah and Sanballat had hired him. For this reason he was hired, that I should be **afraid** and act that way **and sin**, so that they might have cause for an evil report, that they might reproach me."* (Nehemiah 6:5-13 – NKJV, emphasis added)

Nehemiah had reason to feel the pressure of fear in this situation. People were talking. What if a bad report did get back to the king? What if there were assassins looking for an opportunity to kill him? What if the prophetic warnings were true?

It is interesting to note that Nehemiah responded out of his identity saying, *"Should such a man as I flee?"* Because he knew who he was, and because what he was doing came out of his confidence in his identity, his *supernatural* reaction was to resist the idea even though it seemed to be coming from a legitimate source (*prophecy*) and sounded spiritual (*Let us meet together in the house of God*).

Nehemiah was also already in a fear-resisting momentum. From the beginning of his mission, those that opposed the mission had been endeavoring to use fear and intimidation against him. In earlier chapters we read of how their enemies laughed at them, mocking and ridiculing their efforts and threatening those that were working on the wall. But, from the beginning, Nehemiah had stayed faithful and the momentum of that faithfulness kept him on track.

As a result, in the face of fear he received revelation. Verse 12 starts out with the words, *"Then I perceived..."* Because Nehemiah was moving in faith, he was able to clearly see what was really going on. He came to understand that if he cooperated with fear, it would lead to sin.

Whenever we act out of fear, we will miss the mark; we will sin. This is the goal of the operating system of the enemy. This is the goal of fear.


### Being Angry

Paul told us to *"Be angry, and do not sin."* (Ephesians 4:26a – NKJV) The insinuation here is that with anger comes the temptation to sin and we must overcome that temptation to miss the mark.

One year for our anniversary, I bought my wife, Lisa, a new stove. It was a Jenn-Air with dual electric ovens and a gas cook top. She loved to cook with gas but bake with electric. I had the store I bought it from deliver it in the afternoon before she got home from work so I could surprise her. After they delivered it they hauled the old dilapidated oven away for no additional charge. I was feeling pretty pleased with myself.

Since we lived in the country, we fueled with propane. The new stove came preset for natural gas so, before we could prepare dinner that evening, I needed to switch out a few parts.

When I got the stove unboxed, I found that the new range I was assembling was missing the kit that changed it from gas to propane. Dang. That's irritating. So, I headed back to the store to report the error thinking all the way there, "I hope these guys don't give me any hassle." (Note here my low-grade fear manifesting as negative anticipation.)

It has been said that, *"Fear is that little darkroom where negatives are developed."*[9] By the time I arrived at the store I had already begun to develop a picture of how things might go and the picture wasn't pretty. I found a young lady in the appliance department and explained what I needed. I probably seemed a little pushy though I really was trying to stay positive.

First, she asked me if I was sure the parts were missing. I assured her that I had looked VERY carefully. Then, she suggested that she could order a kit for me. I patiently explained that my old stove was gone and my wife would be coming home soon so I needed to finish the conversion in order to complete the surprise. There was another stove like mine sitting there so I suggested that I could just take the kit from it. Problem solved, right? Not so fast! She said she could not do that because that would make the one on the floor defective. "Oh," I said, "but it's OK that the range your company just sold me *is* defective?" I

---

[9] *Pritchard, Michael*

could feel my temperature rising.

Then she suggested that I could just bring the whole range back in and exchange it. "The whole range?" I questioned. "That would be stupid." You can ask anybody who knows me and they will testify that I'm not a quiet person. My normal volume is already above average so by this time I suspect I was getting pretty loud. I wasn't really super angry but I am sure that poor girl couldn't tell.

I was just *afraid* that it would be days before we could use the new range and that my surprise was going to go down in flames. The temptation that was accompanying my anger was working hard to push me over the edge. The young woman was getting frustrated too. I'm sure she had a few basic rules taught to her by the store and she was "afraid" to do the wrong thing. Thankfully, another more experienced employee intervened and immediately provided me with what I needed.

Now, if you're thinking that I was in the right, you're missing the point. Any time that we are acting out of fear, we are not acting out of love. The fear that was working in me may seem minor, but it clearly was keeping me from being an effective witness to at least one young lady. I wonder how many times this happens in the lives of Christians every day?

### Fear and Anger

I believe that the vast majority of anger is a result of fear. The two are often associated in the scripture.

David's older brother, Eliab, was angry with David for asking about the reward for slaying Goliath. (1 Samuel 17:28) Is it possible that Eliab might have been afraid that his crazy little brother might get himself killed because he didn't have the sense to stay away from the giant? (Or, Eliab could have been afraid that David might just win and then they'd all look silly for not dealing with the giant themselves.)

In chapter 18 of 1 Samuel, the women who came out to meet the victorious armies of Israel were singing, *"Saul has slain his thousands, and David his ten thousands."* The very next verse tells us that Saul became angry. Saul said, *"Now what more can he have but the kingdom?"* Not only does this verse show fear but in verse 12 of the same chapter is says, *"Now Saul was afraid of David because the Lord was with him, but had departed from Saul."* (1 Samuel 18:7, 8, & 12 – NKJV) This also illustrates the connection between fearlessness and the Spirit, which I spoke of in chapter 1. Here the Spirit has departed and fear has entered in. (v 12)

David wasn't immune to problems with anger and fear. David struggled with it when Uzzah died after touching the Ark. 2 Samuel 6:8-9 tells us that David was both angry and afraid.

Our own anger can be a strong indicator of the presence of fear. I remember being a little child, about four years old, and having my grandma get very angry at me. It was a real shock to my little mind because Grandma had NEVER been angry with me before. I just couldn't understand why she was yelling at me and spanking me! All I had done was cross the busiest street in our neighborhood (without looking) to see what my older brother was doing at a neighbor's house. What was the *big deal*?

Anyone reading this **knows** what the *big deal* was. Looking back, I'm just glad that Grandma didn't have a heart attack. I gave her quite a scare and the experience made me afraid too. Unfortunately, I didn't become afraid of crossing the street. I became afraid of Grandma! I did get over it but it took a while.

Fear had caused her to act outside of her normal disposition toward me. Someone might say, "Rightly so!" But her goal, keeping me safe, was not accomplished. I still didn't understand that I wasn't supposed to cross the street but I was now aware to watch out for Grandma.

Making Grandma angry was easy. All I had to do was get beyond her ability to take care of me. It scared her. Now, think with me. Is it possible for me to scare God? Is it possible for me to get beyond His ability to take care of me?

**Is God Angry?**

So much of Christianity has been deceived by an idea that the God of love is angry most of the time. I was once on a show at a Christian television station where viewers could call in and ask questions of a panel of pastors. A young man called in and said that he felt far away from God and unworthy to come to Christ.

I responded that God loved him and had a wonderful plan for his life. I told him several things to help him understand that he could come to Jesus just as he was and be welcomed just as the prodigal son was welcomed back by his father in Luke 15. I ended with the statement "God is in a good mood."

Just then another pastor chimed in. The first thing he said was, *"God is angry with the wicked every day."* (Psalm 7:11b, KJV)

Consider these translations of Psalm 7:11:

> *God is a righteous judge, a God who displays His wrath every day.* (New International Version)

> *God is a fair judge, a God who is* **angered by injustice** *every day.* (GOD'S WORD Translation,

emphasis added)

> *God [is] a righteous judge, And He **is not** angry at all times.* (Young's Literal Translation, emphasis added)

Love isn't just an aspect of God's personality. Love is the essence of His being. God is love! (1John 4:8) 1 Corinthians 13:5 tells us that love is not provoked or in the words of the New International Version "is not easily angered". God is against injustice at all times but is He is not *angry* all of the time. Paul said:

> *This is a faithful saying and worthy of all acceptance, that Christ Jesus came into the world to save sinners, of whom I am chief.* (1 Timothy 1:15 – NKJV)

Paul didn't say, *"I was chief"*. He used the present tense *"I am chief"*. Paul recognized that he was still an imperfect person, a person still not perfectly on the mark every time. Paul also recognized that God sent His Son to *save* sinners. So, was God angry at Paul everyday? Indeed, is God angry most of the time? If God's primary focus is on the injustice and wickedness in the world, then we would have to conclude that a moment cannot go by when God is not steaming mad. With over seven billion people in the world, somebody somewhere is screwing up right now! But since Jesus is our model of how the Father reacts toward sin, I think we need to remember the story of the woman caught in adultery:

> *"Now early in the morning He came again into the temple, and all the people came to Him; and He sat down and taught them. Then the scribes and Pharisees brought to Him a woman caught in adultery. And when they had set her in the midst, they said to Him, "Teacher, this*

*woman was caught in adultery, in the very act. Now Moses, in the law, commanded us that such should be stoned. But what do You say? This they said, testing Him, that they might have something of which to accuse Him. But Jesus stooped down and wrote on the ground with His finger, as though He did not hear. So when they continued asking Him, He raised Himself up and said to them, "He who is without sin among you, let him throw a stone at her first." And again He stooped down and wrote on the ground. Then those who heard it, being convicted by their conscience, went out one by one, beginning with the oldest even to the last. And Jesus was left alone, and the woman standing in the midst. When Jesus had raised Himself up and saw no one but the woman, He said to her, "Woman, where are those accusers of yours? Has no one condemned you?" She said, "No one, Lord." And Jesus said to her, "Neither do I condemn you; go and sin no more."* (John 8:2-11 – NKJV)

Who exemplifies the heart of the Father in this passage, Jesus or the people quoting scripture? That was the same problem we had on the television show. While the pastor knew the scripture, he had somehow missed the heart of the Father. What is even more amazing is that the pastor missed the mark! His fear of sin caused him to sin. Thank God the other pastors on the panel picked up the "fumbled ball" with their answers and encouraged the young man to come to Jesus.

The fear connected with sin makes us behave outside the nature of who God created us to be. We cannot and must not focus on sin. As we focus on "hitting the mark", the fear of sin loses its power and we find that we are able to "STOP IT" and move in greater levels of victory over sin.

# Chapter 6

## Obediphobia – Fear of Obedience

*He doesn't want you to obey a bunch of rules, He wants your love.*

*-- Lacey Mosley – Flyleaf*

Are you afraid to obey? While most people would not say they have fear associated with obedience, most of us would admit that the idea of having to obey someone doesn't exactly conjure up the most pleasant thoughts. For most of us, obedience was something we did because we *had to*, not because we *wanted to*.

Obediphobia manifests itself in a fear of structures, systems, and rules. The obediphobe feels trapped, forced to conform.

Order becomes anxiety and as the anxiety increases, the obediphobe looks for a way of escape.

Let's look at a couple of cursory definitions.

Obedience

> 1. The state or quality of being obedient.
>
> 2. The act or practice of obeying; dutiful or submissive compliance: Military service demands obedience from its members.
>
> 3. A sphere of authority or jurisdiction, ***especially ecclesiastical***. (Emphasis added)

*Especially ecclesiastical!* I find it interesting that this basic definition of the word (found at dictionary.com) connects obedience to the idea of church. It sees obedience as dutiful and compliant. If the church is the people of God and the world sees obedience as something that makes them less than comfortable, then that might explain why people outside (and some inside) the church struggle with a fear of obedience. Here's another word we need to define.

Obey

> 1. To comply with or follow the commands, restrictions, wishes, or instructions of: to obey one's parents.
>
> 2. To comply with or follow (a command, restriction, wish, instruction, etc.).
>
> 3. (Of things) to respond conformably in action to: The car obeyed slightest touch of the steering wheel.

Again, look at the words used to define this concept. We see commands and restrictions. Most people aren't in love with being told what to do and feel limited by the idea of restrictions.

Do these perceptions about obedience affect our thoughts and attitudes toward faith and people of faith? More importantly, how do these attitudes affect our hearts toward God?

What if I told you that biblical obedience looked much different than the definitions given up to this point in this chapter? What if people are Obediphobic because they don't really understand God's idea of obedience?

Let's look at an early example of obedience in the Bible:

> *In your seed all the nations of the earth shall be blessed, because you have obeyed My voice."* (Genesis 22:18 NKJV)

Do you know what act of obedience Abraham did to have God say this to him? Abraham obeyed God by taking his son, Isaac, and preparing to offer him as a sacrifice. In fact, Abraham was at the point of raising the knife when God stopped him. The Hebrew word translated "obeyed" in this text is the word "shama".

This is the first time the word "shama" is translated "obey" in the New King James Version of the Bible. When I realized this fact, I began to wonder. Was it possible that from Adam to Abraham, obedience was an unnecessary idea? That couldn't be right could it?

I looked on biblegateway.com and found that in most of the translations of the Bible, this was indeed the first place the Hebrew word "shama" was translated into some form of the English word "obey". But, it was not the first time the word "shama" was used in the Bible. So how is "shama" translated elsewhere? Here is the first use of the word "shama" in the Bible:

> *They **heard** the sound of the LORD God walking in the garden in the cool of the day, and the man and his wife hid themselves from the presence of the LORD God among the trees of the garden.* (Genesis 3:8 NKJV Emphasis added)

In this verse the word "shama" is translated *heard*. When they heard God, though they weren't initially compliant (they tried to hide), they did "shama". How can that be? This shows us something important about the way God views obedience. Let's look at another verse:

*The angel of the LORD said to her further, "Behold, you are with child, And you will bear a son; And you shall call his name Ishmael, Because the LORD has* **given heed** *to your affliction.* (Genesis 16:11 NKJV Emphasis added)

Here, God is speaking to Hagar, Sarah's handmaiden. Where is the word "shama" here? It is translated in this text as "given heed". And who was giving heed? The Lord! And what did the Lord "obey"? Did God obey Hagar's affliction? (Let's not be silly!)

Are you confused yet? Don't be. The problem we have is that we think of obedience as compliance to something that is being *forced* on us. The "shama" that God is looking for is a hearing response to his voice. God is much more interested in relationship with us than He is mechanical compliance by us. That's why He laments:

*Therefore the Lord said: "Inasmuch as these people draw near with their mouths And honor Me with their lips, But have removed their hearts far from Me, And their* **fear** *toward Me is taught by the commandment of men,* (Isaiah 29:13 – NKJV, emphasis added)

God looks on the heart. So if He says, "Sit down" and you reply, "I'm sitting down on the outside but I'm standing up on the inside" your compliance was NOT biblical obedience. God didn't create us just so He could have someone to order around. If God only desires compliance, He would easily be able to instantly force the world to do His will.

## We Were Created for Relationship

When Abraham was prepared to sacrifice Isaac, the Bible says that he did so knowing that God, his Friend, would raise Isaac from the dead.

> *By faith Abraham, when he was tested, offered up Isaac, and he who had received the promises offered up his only begotten son, of whom it was said, "In Isaac your seed shall be called," concluding that God was able to raise him up, even from the dead, from which he also received him in a figurative sense.* (Hebrews 11:17-19 – NKJV)

Relationship was the key to Abraham's ability to hear (obey) God.

When my son Joshua was five, I had to take him to the doctor to get an immunization shot. He was, at that point, old enough to figure out what was about to happen and, needless to say, he wasn't happy.

He didn't like shots. (I don't blame him for not liking shots; I don't like them either.) But, I knew that the small amount of pain he was potentially going to experience was nothing compared to the possible consequences of not having that immunization.

We tried to explain to him that he needed the shot. Then the nurse showed me how to sit him on my lap and put my arms around him in such a way as to enable her to get to his arm from behind. While his arm was held securely, his legs were not. He kicked and screamed and inflicted quite a bit of discomfort to my shins.

While Josh was doing that the nurse slipped behind us and quickly injected the required dosage. As Joshua continued to kick and scream, the nurse came back to the front and said, "OK, we're all done!" Josh, however, continued to kick and scream. Next, I said, "Josh! We're done." He paid no attention to either of us and kicked and screamed some more. Finally, he stopped and started looking at his arm. He had been kicking and screaming so hard that he hadn't even felt the shot! You know those times when we tell our children, "This is going to hurt me more than it will you"? That time it was TRUE!

As adults, we have come to understand that there are things we have to do that may not be easy, but we choose to do them because we are looking toward a greater good. This is true of all loving parents, including our Heavenly Father.

Abraham had such an amazing relationship with God that he knew that God, his Friend, wouldn't ask him to do something that wasn't totally worth the pain it might cause. Abraham didn't just believe *in* God, Abraham believed *God*. Abraham didn't simply comply with God's wishes. Abraham came into agreement with his Friend that he trusted.

So, let's think together. What does the Bible say God is? *"God is love."* (1 John 4:8 – NKJV) Can God do anything that is outside the nature of who He is? Not unless He is schizophrenic. (Some Christians seem to serve a schizophrenic God but I prefer not to.)

So, when God carries out justice, it is based in His nature. When He pours out His wrath it is always in line with love. Have you ever exercised your wrath on a bee that was endangering your child? Then you somewhat understand the wrath of God. It is not the bee itself that is the object of your wrath as much as it is the bee's potential to harm your child that has brought swift action. I like bees because I like honey. But I have swatted a few bees because they got too close to my children.

Now, let's think together a little more. This God who is the embodiment of love, loves us, right? And, this loving God wants a relationship with us. He wants us to "shama" Him. He wants us to hear His voice and He wants us to respond positively to that voice for *our good*.

This is where we have misunderstood obedience. Most of us have had someone force us into compliance for their benefit, not ours. That is *not* who God is.

Bill Johnson likes to say, *"God can't think of something stupid for you to do".* If God is asking you to do something, He is looking for an opportunity to bless you not simply control you!

I illustrated this one Sunday morning to our congregation. First, I asked for two volunteers. Then I asked them if they would be willing to lie down on the floor in front of the congregation and stick their heads under two chairs that I had set where everybody could see them.

I encouraged them that they would be blessed if they did. What I didn't tell them was that there was a twenty-dollar bill taped under each chair. As each of the volunteers came into agreement with my voice, they came into a place of being able to receive the benefit I had planned for them. Fear wants us to avoid obedience because fear wants to keep us from the place of blessing and fulfillment that God is longing to take us to.

Let's try another illustration:

Have you ever given directions to someone on how to get somewhere only to have them take what they thought was a shortcut and get lost? I've given specific directions to individuals because I was wanting them to *avoid* construction only to have them show up late because *they* thought *they* knew the area and *they* thought *their* way would get them to our meeting more quickly.

In July of 2010 our church hosted a Firestorm Conference with Kevin and Chad Dedmon. At the same time, the state of Ohio had just finished a new four-lane version of route 24. Our church is located on the road that used to be route 24. When they made the change, our address changed from 20000 US 24 to 20000 County Road 424.

We told people who were coming to the conference NOT to use their GPS. They did not obey. They ended up lost. We had sent out maps and directions. They trusted their GPS more than they trusted us. When their GPS failed, they called and heard the right voice, which led them to our location.

If they had "obeyed" it would have made their life better. Was I trying to control them? NO! And God is not trying to control us! Obedience to God isn't "us" complying with a dictatorial monster. Obedience is "us" in relationship with a loving Father who knows us better than we know ourselves.

Listen carefully to what I am about to say. **God would never ask you to do something that you don't want to do.** He may ask you to do something you THINK you don't want to do, but your "stinking thinking" doesn't change the reality of what God knows. He knows what you were created to do and there is nothing more fulfilling than doing what we were made to do.

He also knows what you weren't designed to do and if He tells you that you shouldn't do something, you definitely don't want to do it. If we can get this it will forever change the way we think about obedience.

If God is asking you to do something, it can't possibly go wrong. If God is asking you, He is only asking you because He wants you to become all that you were created to be.

Did God trick Jesus into coming to earth to die on the cross? NO! So, did Jesus know that He was coming here to die for our sins? YES!! Then that means the passion of Christ was something He wanted to do! How could Jesus *want* to do what He did?

> *Looking unto Jesus, the author and finisher of our faith, who for the joy that was set before Him endured the cross, despising the shame, and has sat down at the right hand of the throne of God.* (Hebrews 12:2 – NKJV)

Jesus knew by faith that the pain He would experience was nothing compared to the glory that would result. If we could just begin to truly see by faith that obedience is always the glorious choice that it is, we would never hesitate to choose the route that God gives us.

If God is asking you to become a missionary to the deepest darkest part of the world, He cannot be mistaken. You *want* to go there even if you haven't realized it yet. In a real sense, God cannot ask you to go to a foreign field because if He is asking you to go there, it has ceased to be foreign. He could never ask anyone to do something that wasn't meant to fulfill the deepest longings of why they were created. So, when He directs you to go someplace different, the place where you currently are has just become *foreign*.

When Lisa (my wife) and I first met, she had made up her mind that she would NEVER marry a pastor. She had grown up in a pastor's home and she did not want to be a pastor's wife. This is not an indictment of the home she grew up in. It was just the reality of the time and culture in which she was raised. Being pastors in the hills of rural Ohio wasn't easy for her parents. It was a low-income area and while most of the people were kind, many of them had experienced hard lives.

When the longhaired Jesus freak (me) showed up at her daddy's Pentecostal church, no one (including me) saw a pastor in the making. I had a good paying job in the big city and, as we felt God's hand directing our union, Lisa felt "safe". But, Jehovah Sneaky had other ideas!

When God's pastoral call on my life became clearer, we both understood that Lisa had been trained her whole life to be the helper I would desperately need if I was going to have any chance of pastoring well. Our first church was down in the hills of southeastern Ohio, not far from where we grew up. We didn't have much and had given up a lot to take that first church but we were actually very happy! I remember Lisa saying that she NEVER wanted to leave that area. (Neither did I.) But once again God had ideas for us that we would have never had for ourselves.

Since then, we have served four other congregations in Indiana and Ohio. At the time of this writing we have lived in northwestern Ohio since 1997. It's *really* flat here! We grew up in the hills and we do sometimes miss them, but being where God wanted us to be has been more fulfilling than our own plans could have ever been.

In 2009, I heard Banning Liebscher, the founder of Jesus Culture; tell the story of how he almost left Bethel Church in Redding, California, to become an intern with another organization. When he was asked to be the Youth Pastor at Bethel he initially refused saying that he did not have a heart for Bethel Church or youth ministry. In the message he spoke that afternoon called *Pressure Free Ministry*, Banning joked that when it comes to our plans, "I don't think God cares". I am so glad that God didn't "care" about Banning's plans. I am glad God helped Banning to stay in Redding and create a ministry that is now touching millions of lives around the world. *I think Banning is too.*

### The Greatest Possible Blessing

When we begin to fully understand that when God asks us to do something He is doing so in order to give us the greatest possible blessing, then we can begin to see obedience as the "easy yoke" Jesus spoke about in Matthew 11:30. If God is asking us to do something, it's because He knows us better than we know ourselves. He knows that deep down, we really *want* to do whatever He is asking.

Fear distorts who God is and what God wants. Fear tells us we *have* to do what God says "or else" and then mocks us if and when we fail. Fear sends temptation our direction to divert us from God's best for us.

In my chapter on the fear of sin I said that temptation is an attempt by the enemy to get us to settle for less than God's best for us. When temptation comes, we are tempted to obtain

98

through *illegitimate* means the very thing that God wants us to receive through *legitimate* means.

The temptation of Christ in Matthew 4 is a perfect example. Nothing that Satan offered was in and of itself illegitimate. Jesus did need food, God had promised protection, and all of the kingdoms of the world were intended by the Father to be Christ's. But what Satan was tempting Jesus to take was the "easy" way. (The truth is that Satan's way leads to slavery and there is nothing easy about it.)

Jesus understood a reality that the greedy devil still can't understand, the reality of the resurrection. When we fully understand the power of the resurrection, temptation loses all of its power. Consider these words of Jesus:

*Most assuredly, I say to you, unless the grain of wheat falls into the ground and dies, it remains alone; but if it dies, it produces much grain.* (John 12:24 – NKJV)

Have your plans and ideas ever had to die? Have your hopes, your dreams, or your desires ever had to be sacrificed? What have any of us ever given up that God cannot give back to us? The reality is that what we have given up is the kernel of corn and what He wants to restore to us is the ear of corn! Sometimes suffering the death of something is the path to ultimate victory.

I believe that if we could truly comprehend the reality of the power of His resurrection, we would never sin. Think about it! Why do we sin? We sin because we have a desire and we don't believe it is going to be met in a legitimate way. As a result of our unbelief, we attempt to get our desire met in an illegitimate way that "misses the mark" (sins). But when we are willing to let that kernel (that won't be enough to satisfy us anyway) fall to the ground and die, then God can multiply it back to us as much more. When we give up what temporarily satisfies, He gives what eternally multiplies!

It is very likely that you have already experienced something like this in your life. For example, have you ever exchanged your plans for the plans of your spouse, your children, or some other family member? (Most of us have done something like this at one time or another.) Did the change of plans then turn out to be much better than you expected? I've (reluctantly) done this many times thinking it was my "duty" to put the desires of my wife and kids ahead of my own desires only to end up getting more benefit out of the change of plans than they did. Instead of a little pleasure for myself, there was multiplied pleasure for all. That's the resurrection reality!

*Then He said to them all, "If any man come after me, let him deny himself and take up his cross daily and follow me.* (Luke 9:23 – NKJV)

Does the Lord ask this of us to destroy us? Does He mean us harm? No, He does this for our benefit. He asks this of us so He can see us positioned for His greater reality.

What have you lost? What are you grieving over? Turn it over to Him and He can bring it back: better, fuller, richer, bigger, and more complete! It's the reality we experience when we lay down our old lives and He gives us new better lives. The obedience we enter into in our new lives brings us into relationship with God and greater relationships with each other. We could never experience this level of relationship outside of relational obedience we have with Him through the Holy Spirit. When we enter into that "shama" relationship with the God who is perfect love, then the fear is cast out and we become joyfully obedient, not begrudgingly compliant.

This concept of a more biblical obedience is transformational. When we see obedience as agreement, we move into that deeper relationship of friendship that Jesus spoke of.

> *"No longer do I call you servants, for a servant does not know what his master is doing; but I have called you friends, for all things that I have heard from My Father I have made known to you."* (John 15:15 – NKJV)

Biblical obedience is a partnership. In partnership, I have a much greater motivation for what I am doing than I do when I am merely a servant.

Fear is doing all it can to keep us from being all that God has created us to be. But as I say "NO" to Obediphobia, I become able to fully recognize the fear that fosters disobedience and "STOP IT" before it robs me of all that God desires for me.

# Chapter 7

# Cherophobia – Fear of Happiness

*God cannot give us a happiness and peace apart from Himself, because it is not there. There is no such thing. -- C. S. Lewis*

Do you know any people who are afraid to be happy? I do. Unfortunately, many of them are Christians.

Cherophobia is the extreme and irrational fear of gaiety or happiness. Those who have this phobia aren't always sad, but they're afraid to express happiness and they are afraid to have fun. Like other phobias, Cherophobia may be caused by a past traumatic or negative experience. It may also be caused by an intense fear of disappointment.

Kris Vallotton, author of *Spirit Wars: Winning the Invisible Battle Against Sin and the Enemy*, has spoken openly about his battle with a foreboding spirit. A foreboding spirit is a spirit that causes people to always expect something bad to happen right after something good happens. Kris tells of being prayed for and someone commanding the foreboding spirit to leave him. At first, he didn't know exactly what to think. He wasn't even aware that there was a foreboding spirit let alone the idea that he might have one affecting him. Within days he realized that his life had changed. We all need to be aware that the enemy wants us to expect something negative in order to enable his devices to steal our happiness.

Some people are so afraid of disappointment that they will literally derail their own happiness in order to protect themselves from the smallest possibility of being disappointed. Even worse, I have seen people sabotage the happiness of their friends and family thinking they are *protecting them* from disappointment.

How about you? Have you ever sabotaged your own happiness out of fear that you might be disappointed? Many of us have. This is clinically called Cherophobia.

There is much written and available about this fear in the secular world. Most Christians who are under the influence of Cherophobia don't even realize it. They just think they are being "sober minded". Many of them have been taught that happiness is a more frivolous attitude and since some Christians believe that they are called to experience much suffering, they operate under the belief that they aren't supposed to pursue happiness.

In light of this feeling among American Christians, I find it interesting to note that the second line of the Declaration of Independence indicates that our founding fathers believed that happiness was a very important thing. Do you remember this from history class?

> *We hold these truths to be self-evident, that all men are created equal, that they are endowed by their Creator with certain unalienable Rights, that among these are Life, Liberty and **the pursuit of Happiness.*** (Emphasis added)

## God's Plan – Your Happiness

I'm going to come back to the pursuit of happiness later in this chapter but first I have a question:

If God wants you blessed, is it okay for you not to be blessed? Most of the time people think of a blessing as something God gives on a specific occasion rather than a state of being. God's blessing wasn't meant to be an occasional booster shot but rather an ongoing experience. Do we really think that when God gives His blessing that He doesn't wish for it to remain? So again, if God wants you blessed, is it OK for you not to be blessed? Most of us would probably say, "No".

Now, let me ask the question using a different word for blessed. If God wants you to be happy, is it OK for you not to be happy?

"Well, that's not the same thing!" you might say. Actually, it is. One of the main words for blessed in the New Testament is better translated "happy".

Are you happy? Have you been happy all day? Have you been happy all week? How about this whole year so far? Should anyone be happy all of the time? Should anyone be *blessed* all of the time? Maybe a better question would be, "Can anyone be happy all of the time?" Most of us know people who seem to be happy most of the time. We sometimes refer to them as "Happy-go-lucky" people. But what if luck has nothing to do with it?

I know that my personal experience is that while I have not been happy every moment of my life, I've been happy a lot and I'm learning to allow myself to be happy more. I really like being happy. I think that being happy is a good idea. Being unhappy is overrated. I don't know about you, but I try to avoid being unhappy. It makes me, well…. unhappy. (Duh) When the person at the checkout says "Have a good day." I usually respond, "It's unavoidable!" Most people smile when they hear it. Some look at me like I'm crazy. If that's what you're thinking, allow me to quote Billy Joel:

> *"You may be right. I may be crazy. But it just may be a lunatic you're looking for!"*[10]

For the record, if this is the day that the Lord has made (Psalm 118:24), and God makes all things good (1 Timothy 4:4, James 1:17), then how can I possibly have a bad day? Things might be bad but it isn't the day's fault!

## The Pursuit of Happiness

There are Christians that are fearful of the pursuit of happiness. For some of them it sounds too much like another concept that has gained popularity in modern America, "If it feels good do it."

While my experience is that most Christians don't live by the "if it feels good do it" model, I have noticed that many avoid doing things that don't feel good. Is that wrong? Or is it wrong for Christians to do things that feel good?

---

[10] Joel, Billy (Musician). (1980). You May Be Right. Glass Houses. Columbia Records. New York, New York.

This also brings up another couple questions: Do actions follow feelings or do feelings follow actions? Which way should it be?

In the early days of the Jesus movement we sang the song, "The Joy of the Lord Is my Strength." One of the lines says:

*"If you want joy you can sing for it."*

Is that doctrinally correct to sing? Does "doing" bring happiness or does happiness bring doing? Should we do "it" if "it" makes us happy?

The truth is that most of us have a core value that doesn't want to do anything that doesn't feel good immediately. So while we might not think of ourselves as "if it feels good do it" people, our behavior is sometimes "if it doesn't feel good, I won't do it".

> *Who then is a faithful and wise servant, whom his master made ruler over his household, to give them food in due season?* **Blessed** *is that servant whom his master, when he comes, will find so* **doing**. *Assuredly, I say to you that he will make him ruler over all his goods.* (Matthew 24:45-47 NKJV, emphasis added)

Pursuing requires doing. I want you to see an association here between two words: doing and blessed.

In the original language of the New Testament, (Greek), the word for blessed (*makarios*) also translates happy. (More about *makarios* a little later.) The original word for doing translates (are you ready for this?) DOING.

It might seem to some that the only reason that doing brought happiness is because of the reward. But that's the point. Doing brings results. Results bring happiness.

The Apostle Paul taught that we would be rewarded for doing:

> *And whatever you do, do it heartily, as to the Lord and not to men, knowing that from the Lord you will*

*receive the reward of the inheritance; for you serve the Lord Christ.* (Colossians 3:23-24 NKJV)

When we do what we do as unto the Lord we enter into our inheritance. While it is true that it is not by our works that we are saved, our inheritance (something that we didn't earn but that was earned by something else's efforts) is accessed by our right attitude in our service of others.

### Its Own Reward

I have found that doing can sometimes be its own reward. After fishing with my uncle Mike a few years ago, a man asked us how the fishing was that day. My uncle responded, "Great". The man then asked how many we had caught to which my uncle responded, "None". The man then asked how the fishing could be great if we didn't catch any. Mike's answer; "You asked me about the fishing, not the catching." For Mike the very activity of fishing had become something that made him happy.

*But He* (Jesus) *said, "More than that, blessed are those who hear the word of God and keep it!"* (Luke 11:28 – NKJV) Happiness comes as we keep doing what we're supposed to be doing.

When Jesus washed the disciples' feet, He told them that they also ought to wash one another's feet. Now, in a day when people wore sandals and walked everywhere, this was a dirty job. And because they walked the same streets where animals traveled, it was a stinky job. In the context of doing this job for His disciples He said:

*If you know these things, blessed are you if you do them.* (John 13:17 – NKJV)

Again, translate blessed to happy. Is washing feet a happy job? It was for Jesus! Jesus knew a level of happiness that the selfish or self-seeking never experience.

*"I have shown you in every way, by laboring like this, that you must support the weak. And remember the*

*words of the Lord Jesus, that He said, 'It is more blessed to give than to receive.' "* (Acts 20:35 – NKJV)

One morning before church as I was preparing to speak on this very subject, I turned the TV on just in time to catch Robert Schuler interviewing Dr. Steven Post, the author of a book entitled, *Why Good Things Happen to Good People*. Dr. Post quoted the passage that I just shared from Acts. I looked up the book on the web to see what was being said about it. Here is the synopsis I found.

> A longer life. A happier life. A healthier life. Above all, a life that matters—so that when you leave this world, you'll have changed it for the better. If science said you could have all this just by altering one behavior, would you? Dr. Stephen Post has been making headlines by funding studies at the nation's top universities to prove once and for all the life-enhancing benefits of caring, kindness, and compassion. The exciting new research shows that when we give of ourselves, especially if we start young, everything from life-satisfaction to self-realization and physical health is significantly affected. Mortality is delayed. Depression is reduced. Well-being and good fortune are increased. In their life-changing new book, Why Good Things Happen to Good People, Dr. Post and journalist Jill Neimark weave the growing new science of love and giving with profoundly moving real-life stories to show exactly how *giving unlocks the doors to health,* **happiness***, and a longer life.* (Emphasis added)[11]

---

[11] Post, Dr. Stephen (2007) Why Good Things Happen to Good People. Retrieved July 22, 2013 from http://www.amazon.com/Why-Good-Things-Happen-People/dp/0767920171

Imagine that! University studies have been done proving that what Jesus said is true. And don't forget, Jesus said that we are happier when we give than when we receive. I experience this every Christmas. When I was a child it was all about what I got for Christmas. But as I grew up it became less and less about what I got and more and more about what I could give. That's why many people try so hard to outdo each other at Christmas.

> *"But be doers of the word, and not hearers only, deceiving yourselves. For if anyone is a hearer of the word and not a doer, he is like a man observing his natural face in a mirror; for he observes himself, goes away, and immediately forgets what kind of man he was. But he who looks into the perfect law of liberty and continues in it, and is not a forgetful hearer but a doer of the work, this one will be **blessed** in what he does."* (James 1:22-25 NKJV, emphasis added)

This one will be **happy** in what he does!!

To increase the amount of blessing I experience in my life I simply need to increase the amount of blessing that I give to others. (Remember, blessing translates happy.) Is my primary goal today to bless or to be blessed? Am I attempting to bless the Lord or am I attempting to be blessed? When it comes to blessing God, is my attitude "if it feels good I'll do it?" If I'm not "in the mood" do I hold my blessing back?

Do we meet together (have church) to bless others or do we primarily go to church to get what we need? Do I lose my blessing (read happiness) when someone sits in my favorite seat? Am I happy (read blessed) to help out in areas of ministry that might mean that I'll miss out on something going on in the main service? Am I asking so many questions that you are starting to feel unhappy? OK, I'll quit for a while.

I realize that there are times when things are going on that make it hard to feel happy. What is really amazing is that Jesus tells us to be happy at some of the oddest times.

## The Perspective of Happiness

A large part of Jesus' most popular sermon was about being happy. Consider the following passage:

> *"And having seen the multitudes, He went up to the mount, and He having sat down, His disciples came to Him, 2 and having opened His mouth, He was teaching them, saying:*
>
> *3 `Happy the poor in spirit -- because theirs is the reign of the heavens.*
>
> *4 `Happy the mourning -- because they shall be comforted.*
>
> *5 `Happy the meek -- because they shall inherit the land.*
>
> *6 `Happy those hungering and thirsting for righteousness -- because they shall be filled.*
>
> *7 `Happy the kind -- because they shall find kindness.*
>
> *8 `Happy the clean in heart -- because they shall see God.*
>
> *9 `Happy the peacemakers -- because they shall be called Sons of God.*
>
> *10 `Happy those persecuted for righteousness' sake -- because theirs is the reign of the heavens.*
>
> *11 `Happy are ye whenever they may reproach you, and may persecute, and may say any evil thing against you falsely for my sake 12rejoice ye and be glad, because your reward [is] great in the heavens, for thus did they persecute the prophets who were before you."* (Matthew

5:1-12 – Young's Literal Translation)

The preceding passage of scripture is commonly known as the Beatitudes. While I'm not going to teach on all of them here, I do want to mention something found in each one.

Take note that each of these phrases starts out with the word "blessed" in nearly every translation available in the English language. (Obviously, the translation I just used is an exception.) Again, the word in the Greek is the word *makarios*. To understand the meaning of this word we can look back at its use in early Greek literature.

> In ancient Greek times, makarios referred to the gods. The blessed ones were the gods. They had achieved a state of happiness and contentment in life that was beyond all cares, labors, and even death. The blessed ones were beings who lived in some other world away from the cares and problems and worries of ordinary people. To be blessed, you had to be a god.

> Makarios took on a second meaning. It referred to the "dead". The blessed ones were humans, who, through death, had reached the other world of the gods. They were now beyond the cares and problems and worries of earthly life. To be blessed, you had to be dead.

> Finally, in Greek usage, makarios came to refer to the elite, the upper crust of society, the wealthy people. It referred to people whose influence and power put them above the normal cares and problems and worries of the lesser folk -- the peons, who constantly struggle and worry

and labor in life. To be blessed, you had to be very rich and powerful.[12]

When Jesus told the regular people that they were blessed, it wasn't something they were used to hearing in relation to their lives. For the elite who thought of themselves as happy, the words of Jesus were just as unusual as they were for the common men. They thought they were "blessed" because of their righteousness and that the poor were not supposed to be "happy" because they had done something wrong. Suddenly, Jesus is telling all sorts of people that they should be happy!

For example, if we look at verses 11 & 12 of Matthew 5, we find ourselves being told to be happy in the face of persecution. In fact, we're not just being asked to have a sense of well-being and contentment, we're being invited to get giddy with joy! Was Jesus serious? Is what He's telling us attainable in our reality?

I personally believe that happiness and unhappiness cannot be based in the same reality. Happiness is unavoidable in one reality and unattainable in the other. Jesus is giving us an invitation to move out of our world into His, to live from heaven toward earth.

> *If then you were raised with Christ, seek those things which are above, where Christ is, sitting at the right hand of God. 2 Set your mind on things above, not on things on the earth. 3 For you died, and your life is hidden with Christ in God. 4 When Christ who is our life appears, then you also will appear with Him in glory.* (Colossians 3:1-4 – NKJV)

---

[12] Stoffregen, Brian (ND). The History of the Word "Makarios" (Blessed). Retrieved July 22, 2013 from *http://www.crossmarks.com/brian/allsaintb.htm*

Ever hear some say, "Get a life!"? Well, I have one. My life is Christ, or at least it's supposed to be. So basically my life is not my own. Hmm, where have I heard that before?

> *Or do you not know that your body is the temple of the Holy Spirit who is in you, whom you have from God, and you are not your own? 20 For you were bought at a price; therefore glorify God in your body and in your spirit, which are God's.* (1 Corinthians 6:19-20 NKJV)

Do you ever wonder, asking yourself, "Why am I not happy?" Could it be that your focus is on the wrong thing? If my life is about me then the only way for me to be happy is for everything to go my way. The problem then is that the focus is on ME.

But if my life is hidden with Christ in God and my life is about Jesus then my focus is on Jesus. If Jesus is my life then what do I need to be happy except Jesus? If Jesus is my life, what could possibly make me unhappy?

We sing things like, "He's all I need" and "all I need is You", but learning to believe it and live it is harder than singing it. Yet, Paul said that he had *learned* it:

> "*I have learned to be content whatever the circumstances. I know what it is to be in need, and I know what it is to have plenty. I have learned the secret of being content in any and every situation, whether well fed or hungry, whether living in plenty or in want. I can do everything through Him who gives me strength.* (Philippians 4:11-13 NKJV)

We quote verse 13 out of context all of the time! In the context, it's about having the strength to be content. What does it mean to be content? It means to be happy and satisfied. The idea that Paul was communicating was that we find our satisfaction in Christ alone.

If I find my satisfaction in Christ, then I always have a reason to be happy. If I find my satisfaction in anything other than Christ, then I will have many opportunities for dissatisfaction, which is accompanied by unhappiness. **When I learn to be content in everything, I can be happy doing anything!**

So what is the "secret" to contentment? Jesus! When my focus is on Him, everything else comes into perspective.

In the summer of 2012, a massive straight line storm called a Derecho came through Ohio. In addition to the usual storm damage to buildings and trees, thousands of people were without power for days, some for over a week.

While the town I live in did not lose power, many of the people in my church who live outside the city limits did lose power and were greatly inconvenienced. For many of these people, losing power means no water from wells in addition to lost food in their freezers and refrigerators. On top of that, the temperature ran over 100 degrees for several of those days. With food issues, no air conditioning, and no running water, many, many people were not "happy".

In our area, thankfully, there was no loss of life. No one suffered from malnutrition. Injuries were few if any. The truth is that while we were greatly inconvenienced, millions around the world live in much worse conditions 24/7 – 365 days a year. It becomes easier to see why we should be happy when things are put in the right *perspective*.

What is amazing to me is how perspective shifts. I have known people who got new jobs with big pay increases. At first, they were so happy with their new jobs. Everything about the new job, the people they worked with and the atmosphere, was better than the last place.

Then, after six months on the job, they suddenly found out that everyone else working with them was making more money then they were. They instantly became unhappy. They went from extremely happy to feeling like they weren't being treated as well as others. They forgot about the reality that they were so much better off than at the other job and started focusing on what they weren't getting. Yes, perspective is a huge part of keeping our happiness. That's why Paul said:

> *"But godliness with contentment is great gain. For we brought nothing into the world, and we can take nothing out of it. But if we have food and clothing, we will be content with that."* (1 Timothy 6:6-8 – NKJV)

"Paul! What are you thinking? I need my stuff! What about my stuff? My car. My toys. My house! Where am I supposed to sleep? Paul, you're being unreasonable!"

Paul was clearly never a teenager. Every parent of a teenager knows how much stuff teenagers have to have. In fact, not only do they need stuff, they NEED the latest and greatest version of the stuff. Not that lame version that is *so last week*.

And the writer of Hebrews reiterates what Paul tells us as to why we should be content:

> *"Be content with what you have, **because** God has said, "Never will I leave you; never will I forsake you."* (Hebrews 13:5 – NKJV, emphasis added)

If I have Jesus, I have life eternal. I have life abundant. I have real life! We so easily forget that life without Him is not life. When we bring Him into the picture, everything else comes into perspective. But the context of this verse says even more:

> *So we say with confidence, "The Lord is my helper;* **I**
> **will not be afraid.** *What can man do to me?"*
> (Hebrews 13:6 – NKJV, emphasis added)

What is the real enemy of happiness and contentment? Fear. Fear manifests itself in many different ways in order to take away my contentment. Fear often will tell me that I'm not going to get what I want. But if all I want is Jesus and I cannot lose Him, then I cannot lose my happiness. Again, as Paul told the Romans:

> *For I am persuaded that neither death nor life, nor angels nor principalities nor powers, nor things present nor things to come, nor height nor depth, nor any other created thing, shall be able to separate us from the love of God which is in Christ Jesus our Lord.* (Romans 8:38-39 – NKJV)

Fear will often try to make me worry about what others are thinking but if all I really care about is what God is thinking about me, then my happiness becomes indestructible. And what does God think of me? There are so many verses that we could use here but let's just look at one:

> *For I know the thoughts that I think toward you, says the LORD, thoughts of peace and not of evil, to give you a future and a hope.* (Jeremiah 29:11 – NKJV)

Who cares what others think? The person who doesn't have their eyes on Jesus, that's who! If I don't have the latest and the greatest of everything and that is what my focus is on, it will become very easy for fear to creep in and steal my happiness. On the other hand, if I know that God is thinking of me and that His thoughts for me are designed to bring me into a good place, then fear retreats in the face of His overwhelming love.

In chapter 5 on Fear of Sin, I told the story of my experience with a pastor on a local call-in television show. The pastor had the idea that God is angry all of the time. If God is angry all of the time then who is this God that Paul is referring to in his first letter to Timothy? Look at how Paul refers to God twice in this letter:

> *That teaching is found in the gospel that was entrusted to me to announce, the Good News from the glorious and* **blessed** *God.* (1 Timothy 1:11 – Good News Translation, emphasis added)

> *His appearing will be brought about at the right time by God, the* **blessed** *and only Ruler, the King of kings and the Lord of lords.* (1 Timothy 6:15 – GNT, emphasis added)

Paul calls God a happy God! Yes, I know it says blessed. Surprisingly, I could not find a single translation that translated *makarios* "happy" in these two verses. Perhaps that fact illustrates something. Is it possible that the western church just has a hard time thinking of God as a happy God? After all, we live in a society whose insurance companies call calamities like floods and storms "acts of God."

### Representing God

If God's own children primarily think of God as something other than happy, should we be surprised that the world thinks it too?

> *Love has been perfected among us in this: that we*

> *may have boldness in the day of judgment;* **because as**
> **He is, so are we in this world.** *There is no fear in*
> *love; but perfect love casts out fear, because fear involves*
> *torment. But he who fears has not been made perfect in*
> *love.* (1 John 4:17-18 – NKJV, emphasis added)

We are His representatives, re-presenting Him to the world. We carry His Gospel (read good news) to this world. Happy people boldly share the good news. Fearful people hold back. Jesus boldly shared the good news. Jesus is still the Good News! *"As He is, so are we."*

We need to ask ourselves, "Are we good news people?" If the answer is, "I'm afraid not" then perhaps we have diagnosed the reason. Is fear keeping us from being made perfect in His love?

> *But if you look closely into the perfect law that sets*
> *people free, and keep on paying attention to it and do not*
> *simply listen and then forget it, but put it into*
> **practice**—*you will be* **blessed** *by God in what you do.*
> (James 1:25 – GNT, emphasis added)

Once again, the word better translated "happy" is translated "blessed" in this passage. As we look at this verse we come to realize that it might take some practice to become the happy people of God in this world. As we begin to practice carrying blessing (happiness) to the world around us, the world will be drawn toward us and more importantly, to Christ.

During the Jesus Movement a singer called Honeytree wrote these lyrics:

> (Verse 1)
>
> *Well, I was out on the street, about nine o'clock,*

*Kicking up my heels, just a-taking a walk,*

*Smiling a smile, singing a song,*

*Kicking up my heels, just chugging along,*

*And wasn't it a shame that I had to stop?*

*I was rudely interrupted by a big old cop, he said...*

*"Kid, anybody as happy as you are has got to be loaded,"*

*And I said, "But officer, you can..."*

(Chorus)

*Rattle me, shake me,*

*Smell my breath and make me roll up both of my sleeves,*

*Search me any way you please, but I'm clean,*

*I got nothing to hide,*

*The only reason I'm happy is because I got the Spirit inside.*

(Verse2)

*Well, I got back home about a quarter to ten,*

*My mama said, "Honey, where have you been?"*

*She said, "I've been reading about this marijuana weed, and anybody as happy as you are has got to be doing something wrong," And I said, "But mother, you can..."* (Chorus)

(Verse 3)

*Well, the very next day, I was off to school,*

*This time I knew I'd better play it cool,*

*So I got to my class, I sat in my place,*

*But I forgot all about that dumb smile on my face,*

*The teacher saw me grinning and she asked me what for,*

*And I just told her I was happy,*

*She marched me out the door, and straight to the principal's office, who sat me down, looked at me said, "I'm sorry, but anybody as happy as you are has obviously been smoking in the boys room." I said, "But sir, I'm a girl!" And you can...* (Chorus)[13]

In the late 1960's and early 1970's, there was a time of upheaval in our nation. A lot of young adults were trying to figure out what life was all about. They had experienced the assassination of a president. The war in Vietnam was killing their friends. Social unrest had caused rioting on many college campuses. Drug overdoses had taken the lives of some of the brightest and best in music and the arts. Barry McGuire was singing about the "Eve of Destruction".

Suddenly, the Jesus People showed up and began sharing the Good News. They initially didn't have any programs or "plan of salvation" tactics. They just had an experience with Jesus. Thousands were swept into the Kingdom. The Jesus Movement was simply full of happy hippies who shared their experience with the world. They were just re-presenting the God that they had experienced.

---

[13] Honeytree, Nancy (Musician). (1975). Rattle Me, Shake Me. Evergreen. Myrrh Records. Word Entertainment. Nashville, Tennessee.

## Helping the Hurting

Do we have a right to be happy when others are miserable? While it has been said that "Misery loves company", do we really believe that we can bring *blessing* (read happiness) to others by joining in their misery? While we don't cavalierly approach those who are going through a tough time, we are not likely to help them by being depressed with them. Paul did tell us to *"mourn with those that mourn"* (Romans 12:15) but what does that look like?

Jesus said that those who mourn should be happy. (Matthew 5:4) Isn't that impossible? No! Not at all. I have seen it many times as a normal part of being a pastor. I have been with many people during the death of a family member who, though they were in mourning, could be happy at the same time.

> Paul said, *"Brothers, we do not want you to be ignorant about those who fall asleep, or to grieve like the rest of men, who have no hope.* (1 Thessalonians 4:13 – NKJV)

We, who have hope of eternal life, have a "blessed assurance" that *can* give us the ability to respond to death differently. I say it *can*, but I also realize that it sometimes doesn't. Fear will often attempt to enter in during these times. I have seen people's sorrow compounded as fear of a life without a loved one tormented them.

The loss of a financial provider, a caregiver, a lover, can be devastating but if we are able to overcome the belief system of fear with the power of love-based faith, our perspective shifts. I have even watched people battle cancer and never lose their happiness!

I've watched a young couple suffer the injustice of losing not one, but two babies. Then they were told that they could never have any more children. Yes, they mourned, but they also kept their sense of well-being, moved on in life, and had happy days. Later, because they were able to keep their focus, they received not one, but two miracle children.

What if they had given in to fear? What if they had gotten angry with God and moved into disappointment and offense? I have seen tragedy like this turn hearts cold and destroy marriages and families.

I have also seen many people turn their hearts to the God that the Apostle Paul calls "Happy" and find breakthrough and freedom. Today is a great day to stop being afraid of happiness. This fear can and must be overcome. Fear itself is at this very moment afraid that you will become terminally happy. May you become dead to past disappointments and alive to the amazing opportunities God has for you on the road ahead!

Don't forget, fear is afraid of you. Resist that devil; he will flee in fear of you! (James 4:7) The enemy will tell you "resistance is futile" but you can joyfully resist and, through resistance, you can "STOP IT!"

# Chapter 8

# Euphobia – Fear of Good News

*Anxiety does not empty tomorrow of its sorrows, but only empties today of its strength -- Charles Spurgeon*

I'm starting to believe that much of the world has a fear of good news. Have you ever heard the old adage, "No news is good news"? Today, it's been reworded: "Good news is no news". It seems that people won't turn on the TV for good news so the news people have become the harbingers of anxiety.

If you want to see Euphobia in action, watch the weather team on your local station when the big storm that is going to hit your area runs out of steam. They are so disappointed. While they will say they're glad the "big one" didn't hit, their body language says otherwise.

Every day there's something new to worry about. Jobs and the economy, new strains of some disease, terrorism; there are so many things to fear.

In 1975 I was graduating from high school. On April 28th of that year Newsweek Magazine had an article predicting another ice age in my lifetime. Nearly forty years later, instead of an ice age, the world is worrying about global warming. (The world may worry but I'm NOT!) Recently, I saw a list of ten things to worry about on the Internet that had "global warming" as number 8 and "ice age" as number 9.[14] (I know, some smart person can probably come up with a way for both to happen but really, these are about as opposite as it gets!)

If there aren't enough big things for you to worry about, maybe we can make a list of the little things; things that don't seem super important but will *scar your kids for life if you forget them*. On second thought, let's don't and say we did.

There are people who seem like they can't live without the drama that comes with anxiety. The reality is, they aren't really living. Many of the people who cover the news seem to have no lives of their own. They live vicariously through the lives of others. If you are a news junkie, or you love the tabloids, it may be true of you as well. For people like this, anxiety (fear) has become a companion, a part of "normal" life.

My reason for writing this goes back to something I said back in chapter 4, "Whatever you tolerate will eventually dominate." A little worry can seem like no big deal but over time it can defeat the Gospel (good news) in areas of our lives and limit our effectiveness for the Kingdom. What many call simple anxiety is really the enemy of the Gospel (the good news).

In the Kingdom, good news is normal. In this life, for many, worry is normal. It is, therefore, our purpose and privilege to be the carriers of change and see *"the kingdoms of this world are become*

---

[14] *http://health.gather.com/viewArticle.action?articleId=* 281474980993499

*the kingdoms of our Lord, and of His Christ!"* (Revelation 15:11 – KJV)

The really good news is that there is much scripture to help us deal with fear in the form of worry and anxiety.

Look at the words of the Psalmist:

> **23** *Search me, O God, and know my heart; Try me and know my anxious thoughts;* **24** *And see if there be any* **hurtful** *way in me, And lead me in the everlasting way.* (Psalm 139:23-24 – NASB, emphasis added)

Let's look at this verse again in another version:

> **23** *Search me, O God, and know my heart; test me and know my anxious thoughts.* **24** *See if there is any* **offensive** *way in me, and lead me in the way everlasting.* (NIV, emphasis added)

Anxious thoughts impose a danger to us. These kinds of thoughts are breeding grounds for ideas that will become hurtful. Who is hurt and offended by anxiety? I have three suggestions:

First, anxiety is hurtful and offensive to each of us individually. It interferes with our ability to trust God and walk in His ways.

> *An anxious heart weighs a man down, but a kind word cheers him up.* (Proverbs 12:25 – NKJV)

We need to recognize anxiety as an enemy to our heart. Anxiety focuses on the problem while faith focuses on the answer. We need to rid our lives of anxiety. I'll talk about how in a minute.

Second, anxiety is hurtful and offensive to those around us. We are representatives of the Kingdom. When we are anxious (full of anxiety) we become carriers of the wrong kingdom.

Anxiousness creates an atmosphere for negativity and negativity increases anxiousness. It's like a big dirty snowball gaining momentum and causing an avalanche. We must and can stand against it. Again we'll talk about how shortly.

Third, anxiety is hurtful and offensive toward faith. God is looking for people of faith. It is impossible to please God without faith. Anxiousness and faith cannot coexist in the same space.

"But I can't help it!" some may say. Really? Then, using the "I can't help it" logic, God is an unreasonable tyrant! God asks us to control something that we can't control. How unfair is that! And it's also stupid. So, God is both unreasonable and stupid! At this point, some of you are becoming very uncomfortable with my tone. In fact, what I just said is kind of offensive.

Did I say offensive? If you are offended at the idea of someone suggesting God is stupid, how do you think that God feels when His children's behavior says the same thing? Isn't our tolerance for the *sin of being anxious* an impediment to a relationship with the God who longs for us to trust Him?

Did I say, "the sin of being anxious"? Yes I did. Anxiousness is "missing the mark".

> *Do not be anxious about anything, but in everything, by prayer and petition, with thanksgiving, present your requests to God. And the peace of God, which transcends all understanding, will guard your hearts and your minds in Christ Jesus.* (Philippians 4:6-7 NIV)

*"Do not be anxious"* is a fairly strong directive. If God told Paul to speak it then I am pretty sure that God believes we are able to do it. God is not unreasonable. He will not ask us to accomplish something that He hasn't given us the ability to perform. As we begin to resist being anxious about anything, we will develop the strength to not be anxious about everything.

The reality is that anxiety will attempt to come upon us but we have at our disposal, the things needed to dispatch it. Paul says that we defeat anxiety by praying, petition, and giving thanks.

Prayer means going to God. The moment we feel anxious, we need to go straight to God. But we like to fix things. So, often when we are anxious we go to what we think is the source of our anxiousness thinking that we can just fix it ourselves. More often than not, however, the real problem is not something external we can simply fix. It is often an internal heart problem and the only real fix is God.

Then there is petition. Have you ever signed a petition? What is a petition? It's a bunch of people agreeing together! Having people who can agree with you in prayer is a very powerful tool in overcoming anxiousness. We must not be afraid to admit anxiousness. That goes back to the Phobophobia we talked about in Chapter 2. If we are afraid to admit that we are struggling with fear then we won't be open to getting the help we need. But when we have people we know and trust to stand with us as we face our fears, agreement becomes a very powerful tool in overcoming those fears.

Perhaps the greatest tool to overcome anxiety is thanksgiving. Thanksgiving refocuses our thinking on something good rather than focusing on the problem. As we begin to think about what God has done (our history with God) and we begin to thank Him, we have a much better chance to regain our perspective so we can see what He is doing in our current situation.

## Perspective Changes the Way We Think.

Look at the words of the psalmist:

> *When I said, "My foot is slipping," your love, O LORD, supported me. When anxiety was great within me, your consolation brought joy to my soul.* (Psalm 94: 18-19 NIV)

David tells us that the consolations of God restore our joy. What are consolations? In the original language, the word translated "consolations" here literally means to change the way we think, or repent. If we recognize that the way we are thinking isn't the way God is thinking and we decide to start thinking the way God says to think, we will be brought out of the anxious place.

After going to college, my son Joshua began working on a security team at a nuclear power plant in Virginia. After about a year and a half, he got an opportunity to join a group called the C.A.F. Team (Composite Adversary Force). This team travels around the country testing the security at nuclear power plants by serving as adversaries in what are called force-on-force drills. Basically, the kid got to play laser tag for a living.

The problem with the position was that it could only give him eighteen months of work after which he would have to either go back to Virginia or find a new job.

When his time with the CAF team was up, he decided to move to Las Vegas where he hoped an acquaintance would be able to help him get on the police force. When that job didn't pan out, Josh looked for other work. He found plenty, but not the kind of work he had hoped for. At one point he was working three part time jobs but still not bringing in the kind of income that he used to earn back at the nuclear power plant in Virginia. After about 6 months, he began to think about going back to Virginia. Josh made some calls and the doors were wide open.

About that same time, Josh was told about another possible job in New Jersey at a different power plant. He applied and was told that they wanted to interview him. This was when things suddenly got complicated.

The people in Virginia called and asked him to return to work on the 25th of August. The people from New Jersey then called and asked him to come for an interview sometime during the week of the 25th. The Virginia job was a guaranteed position but the New Jersey job could possibly pay more and sounded like it had more potential for upward movement.

The next thing I know, I'm on the phone with a very anxious young man. But that is just the point. I am so glad he called. Why? Because together we were able to help Josh refocus (repent) and start thinking the way God would want him to think.

After reminding him that his steps were ordered by the Lord (Psalm 37:23) and that in all things, God was working toward his good (Romans 8:28), he began to see the amazingly good news that doors of opportunity were opening for him. He was no longer anxious. Instead, he was laughing with me about the whole situation. In the process of praying, he included another believer (me) and therefore created the dynamic of petition. Together we prayerfully and scripturally got the mind of God (repentance) and soon we were thanking God together for His promises.

This is where it got really cool. Joshua then calmly called the people in New Jersey and explained the situation. He told them that he would be leaving Las Vegas to drive back to the east coast on Wednesday the 20th so that he could start work on Monday the 25th and that he didn't know when he would be able to drive up to New Jersey for an interview.

Their immediate response was, "Let us fly you here for an interview on the Friday before you go back to work. Then, we'll fly you to Virginia." It was perfect! Joshua had been dreading the drive. He also had been wondering whether his old car would even make it. Even more amazing, Josh had a friend in Virginia who had a good used car that Josh had been planning to buy anyway!

The very situation that had caused anxiousness when seen through the fearful lenses of the wrong belief operating system had brought blessing when viewed through the right belief operating system. Ultimately, the job in New Jersey turned out to not be a job that Josh even wanted but God still used them to bless Josh and get him back to his great job in Virginia.

I'm not saying that you'll never have any anxious moments. What I am saying is that they can be *moments*. Rather than having anxious days and nights we can through prayer, petition and thanksgiving bring in the peace that will guard our hearts and minds.

Remember, however, that if you want the peace that "transcends" understanding then there will be times that you will have to be willing to give up your right to understand. If I demand to understand then I cannot receive the peace that *passes* (goes beyond) my understanding.

### Long Term Anxiousness

For the purpose of this writing, I am going to define worry as the ongoing practice of being anxious. When anxious moments are extended almost indefinitely we are worrying. Jesus talked about worry:

> *"Therefore I say to you, do not worry about your life, what you will eat or what you will drink; nor about your body, what you will put on. Is not life more than food and the body more than clothing? 26 Look at the birds of the air, for they neither sow nor reap nor gather into barns; yet your heavenly Father feeds them. Are you not of more value than they? 27 Which of you by worrying can add one cubit to his stature?*
>
> *28 "So why do you worry about clothing? Consider the lilies of the field, how they grow: they neither toil nor spin; 29 and yet I say to you that even Solomon in all his glory was not arrayed like one of these. 30 Now if God so clothes the grass of the field, which today is, and tomorrow is thrown into the oven, will He not much more clothe you, O you of little faith?*

*31 "Therefore do not worry, saying, 'What shall we eat?' or 'What shall we drink?' or 'What shall we wear?' 32 For after all these things the Gentiles seek. For your heavenly Father knows that you need all these things. 33 But seek first the kingdom of God and His righteousness, and all these things shall be added to you.*
(Matthew 6:25-33 – NKJV)

The central message of this text is the really good news that our heavenly Father knows what we need! When He says we don't need to worry, then we can KNOW that we don't need to worry.

Worry functions in the mind's eye; our imagination. As we worry we are developing pictures about something bad happening. It has been said that if we know how to worry, then we know how to meditate. Meditating on the good that God says He wants for us is worry in reverse.

We often worry that our little aches and pains are getting worse. What would happen if we began to worry (or imagine) they are getting better? Are we ever tempted to think that nothing can go right for us? How about imagining that because God is on our side, nothing can go wrong?

*And we know that in all things God works for the good of those who love Him, who have been called according to His purpose.* (Romans 8:28 NIV)

God is working! Think about that for a moment. When God starts to do a work, what can resist what HE has decided to do? Next, think about what He is working to accomplish. He is working for our good! Imagine what that looks like. He is not working to punish us. He's working to bless us. He is good. When God does "good" it's really good. When we learn to meditate on how good God is then we will begin to see how good everything He does is.

This is an area of Euphobia that many people struggle with, even Christians. They think that God is behind all things. God is not the doer of all things. God does not do evil. But IN all things, God works. You might even say that God works "in spite" of many things. He knows the good He has done and wants to do.

For many people the idea that God is good is hard to envision. They've heard so much about His wrath (and have imagined themselves to be so deserving of it) that they have a very hard time picturing how very good He wants to be to them. They are literally afraid that the idea of a good God is "too good to be true".

The world has been trained to think of God as this angry being who must and will exact His judgment on everything and everyone. Insurance companies call calamities "acts of God". It's as if God is in heaven playing an elaborate game of "Gotcha" just waiting for us to mess up. It's as if God was saying, "I'll get you my pretty. And your little dog Toto too!"[15]

God isn't angry about our sin because our obedience benefits Him. What does God need from us? He is angry about our sin because of the effect that it has on us! He is angry because our disobedience hurts us.

Most of us are very familiar with Romans 6:23:

> "For the wages of sin is death, but the gift of God is eternal life in Christ Jesus our Lord."

For a lot of people, even Christians, this verse is understood as kind of a "gotcha" verse. The tendency is to focus on the first half of the verse to communicate the idea that "you're going to get what you deserve" when you sin. While it is true that none of us is sinless and based on our own merits we wouldn't deserve everlasting life, there is a misunderstanding that has happened in the thinking of too many people.

---

[15] Spoken by the Wicked Witch of the West in the Wizard of Oz

When we primarily focus on the wages of sin, we develop a line of thinking that says that God wants people to get what they deserve. So, allow me to pose the question, "Does God want us to get what we deserve?" I don't believe He does. If God wanted us to get what we deserve then why send Jesus to die for us? If God wanted us to get what we deserve then His best option would have been to sit back and *let* us get what we deserve. So this verse is not saying, "You get what you deserve". This verse is God saying, "Hey, don't do that sin thing because it's really going to cost you big-time!

Let's examine the wording in this verse a little closer:

Wages, *opsonion* in the Greek language, was a soldier's pay, allowance, or rations. The word actually comes from a Greek word for fish. It was the practice of the culture of that day to pay people with food. Often, Roman soldiers were paid with fish that they immediately consumed. One commentator described it as something to be eaten with bread.[16] Wages were sandwiches!

The word for "death" in this verse is always translated "death" in the New Testament except in the Book of Revelation. There it is twice translated "pestilence". We need to remember that for the people of that day, death was more often a slow painful process rather than an instantaneous ending of life.

The picture of death that Paul is giving us in Romans 6:23 looks a lot like the slow painful death of food poisoning. God is saying, "If you eat this, it'll kill ya!" or in other words, the consumption of sin brings suffering that will ultimately ruin your life. God is not looking forward to making sure you get some kind of payback for your sin. He's trying to encourage us to avoid the consequences of our sin. Now, that is good news!

Even better news is that God is looking to give you a gift! *"But the gift of God is eternal life."* Now what is that? It's favor.

---

[16] THAYER'S GREEK LEXICON, Electronic Database. Copyright © 2002, 2003, 2006, 2011 by Biblesoft, Inc.

God wants you to live life in the atmosphere of His favor. As we live in that favor we experience "eternal life" in the here and now.

This "life" is eternal from the perspective that once it starts it continues. It's not life we receive some day in eternity but it's life that begins now and continues for eternity. We already have it and we are being invited to walk in it everyday! Let's look at verse 22 of Romans 8 for some context:

> But now you are free from the power of sin. You have become a servant for God. Your life is set apart for God-like living. The end is life that lasts forever. (Romans 6:22 NLV)

God finds no great personal benefit in condemning us for our sins. He wants to see us free from our sins so that we can really live! He wants us to experience God-like living! Not that we will be God but that we will experience the kind of life God always intended for us. Remember, it's the goodness of God that leads to repentance. (Romans 2:4)

### What about God's Wrath?

Someone may say, "But what about His wrath?" Good question. Does God pour out His wrath in order to change minds? Some believe it but I don't. Look at this scripture:

> **8** Then the fourth angel poured out his bowl on the sun, and power was given to him to scorch men with fire. **9** And men were scorched with great heat, and they blasphemed the name of God who has power over these plagues; **and they did not repent** and give Him glory. **10** Then the fifth angel poured out his bowl on the throne of the beast, and his kingdom became full of darkness; and they gnawed their tongues because of the pain. **11** They blasphemed the God of heaven because of their pains and their sores, **and did not repent** of

*their deeds.* (Revelation 16:8-11 – NKJV, Emphasis added)

What was the result when God poured out His wrath in this text? They blasphemed (cursed in the NIV) God and they did NOT repent.

God knows that His wrath is not a tool for changing the way people think. He doesn't use His wrath that way. He does everything He can to get us to repent and then when it is clear that we are not going to, He pours out His wrath. When that moment comes, the time to change our minds is long gone.

This truth can be applied to how we treat our children. We often think that "cracking down" on our children is the best way to get them to do what is right. But here is the real question: Did we change the way they think or just the way that they behave? Using force can change the way our children behave for a season but when we change behavior without changing the thought processes that go with that behavior, the unwanted behavior usually returns later in another form.

Goodness, kindness, love, gentleness and the like are all part of the same family and they each have their opposites.

> *Let all bitterness, wrath, anger, clamor, and evil speaking be put away from you, with all malice. And be kind to one another, tenderhearted, forgiving one another, even as God in Christ forgave you.* (Ephesians 4:31-32 – NKJV)

As parents, do we want our children to simply behave because they have to or do we want them to grow up having an understanding of doing what is right? Wouldn't we rather that they do good because it is so much better than the alternative? God doesn't want any of us to do what we do because we have to. He wants us to be mature enough to do what we do because we want to! If God doesn't use His wrath to change the way that people think, what makes us think that it will work for us?

> *A soft answer turns away wrath, but a harsh word*

*stirs up anger.* (Proverbs 15:1 – NKJV)

When we keep ourselves in a place of love and answer accordingly, wrath becomes unnecessary. When we move into fear and answer harshly, our anger is stirred and wrath becomes unavoidable. This is why Paul told the Ephesians to put anger, and its companions, away. (Ephesians 4:31)

I find that when I get angry (freaked out, frustrated, aggravated, agitated, mad), if I ask myself what I might be afraid of, just about 100% of the time I can find something that is fear-based in my thinking. I become angry because I'm afraid something I want or highly value is being threatened.

Let's use the parent-teenager relationship again as an example:

Parents, when your teenager places a high value on their plans and you tell them "No", they may react in fear and become angry because they are not getting what they want. Responding to them angrily only reinforces their negative attitude.

Teenagers, when you freak out and get angry you will not change the way your parents think. You might temporarily get them to give in to your wishes, but you will also create an atmosphere in which they will become more and more resistant. You will in fact reinforce the way they think. Then when something really important comes up, your plans may get shot down just because the way they have come to think and feel about your behavior has brought them to a place of wrath.

*And you, fathers, do not provoke your children to wrath, but bring them up in the training and admonition of the Lord.* (Ephesians 6:4 – NKJV)

Our children can be brought to a place of wrath as well. There is little benefit in forcing a child to behave while they're "under my roof" if the second they leave, they do all the things that I would never let them do. I must help my children learn to think right, not just to do right "because I said so". If I fail to do this then I may have won the battle but I will have lost the war.

While I'm on the subject, let me encourage you parents to never say "because I said so". More often than not, this is a fear-based statement. Making a fear-based decision for your children is never a good decision for your children or you. If you sense the possibility of danger, take a moment to think it through. Teaching them to properly react to danger is wisdom but teaching them to react in fear is foolish.

> *For out of the overflow of the heart the mouth speaks.*
(Matthew 12:34b NIV)

We can learn a lot about what we really believe by listening to what we say. If we are angrily yelling and screaming or grumbling and complaining we need to step back and realize that we are not making things better. Rather, we are likely justifying the thinking of the person whose mind we hope to change. In fact, in moments like this, we need to realize it's very likely that it is *our* mindset that needs to change.

When we start to believe that we can "overcome evil with good" (Romans 12:21) then we will begin to overcome our fear of good news. Instead of being tempted to use threats and coercion, we will be able to use positive information to create positive mental "formations" that will change the way we process thought and assist us in changing the way others think. The best way to get others to experience God's goodness is to apply heavy amounts of His goodness to our own lives and then go and rub others the right way!

Some may think that focusing on God's goodness is somehow short-changing His righteousness and justice. God does indeed demand righteousness and justice, but His righteousness and justice always proceed out of His nature. God is love. It is fear itself that desires to make the focus of the Gospel about something other than who He is.

For much of the history of the church, a sort of fear of good news has caused us to miss the heart of God. As a result, we've displayed a "you better straighten up or God is gonna get you" attitude. God isn't looking for opportunities to punish. He's looking for people upon whom His incredible favor can rest! He's looking for people who can enter into everlasting life now and move into greater and greater levels of it until the day comes when they are consumed by it.

He's not looking to break you; He's looking for your breakthrough. He wants to take you from glory to glory to glory! He's not pointing His finger demanding, "You better…". He's motioning to you to come and experience a better you!

The devil's greatest fear is an army of believers who will reject a "gospel" of doubt and start shouting the good news; a people who will wipe out worry by meditating on His goodness, which is manifest everyday. (Lamentations 3:22-23) It is our destiny to become a host of people who will declare "STOP IT" to the anxiety and depression that plagues the information age.

# Chapter 9

# Xenophobia – Fear of the Unknown

*Avoiding danger is no safer in the long run than outright exposure. The fearful are caught as often as the bold. -- Helen Keller*

Every spring during the season when colleges and universities have spring break, the Bethel School of Supernatural Ministry sends hundreds of students out on mission teams to locations all over the world. These teams go out and do "Firestorms" everywhere they go. A "Firestorm" is a meeting where the presence of God is released for people to be saved, healed, and delivered. Words of knowledge, prophecy and healing prayer are central to these meetings.

Many of the students who attend BSSM are from outside the United States and have visas that won't permit them to travel too often in and out of our country. In order to enable these students to go on mission trips, the school sets up trips inside the U.S. as well. This also helps students who are from the U.S. but can't quite afford the trips to other countries. As a result, our church was blessed to have a "missions team" from Redding come to us in Defiance, Ohio, in March of 2009.

At that point in time, our church had already become immersed in revival culture. We had been in relationship with Bethel Church for about four years so we were pretty comfortable with the kind of ministry we expected them to bring. Prophecy, words of knowledge, healing prayer, signs and wonders had become an expected part of our regular meeting experience. We expected to have our level of experience increased as a result of their visit and we certainly weren't disappointed. The meetings were wonderful. They were naturally supernatural!

### Outside the Christian Comfort Zone

Perhaps you are reading this and you aren't at all comfortable with the idea that supernatural experiences are actually happening in the world today. Perhaps you've been led to think that they happen but not to Christians. Let me encourage you to not let a mild case of Xenophobia keep you from reading more. You can reach the end of this chapter and disagree with its contents completely if you wish. But, you might just find some understanding that will equip you to overcome any fear of the unknown that might be lurking about, even if we don't see eye-to-eye on everything.

During those meetings with the Redding team, we saw some amazing healings. One woman received a healing in her sense of smell. For 55 years she had almost no sensitivity to smell but during one of the services she suddenly could smell everything! She literally went around sniffing people, just rejoicing that she could smell their various colognes and perfumes.

Another lady had come to the meeting but was unable to stand for very long because of intense pain in the heels of her feet. As a result of a word of knowledge, she received prayer and her pain left completely. Shoulders, knees, backs, headaches, and many other ailments were touched by God's presence during those meetings.

Many other people were powerfully touched by prophetic words spoken over their lives. I didn't know all of the people attending because we had quite a few visitors but all of the prophetic words spoken over the folks from our church were amazing. If I had attempted to make a list and tell the team what to say it could not have been as accurate as the things that the Holy Spirit was giving to the students who ministered.

As I said, all of these things were in line with the type of ministry that we had already been experiencing at our church. But then they did *it*. The Redding team did something a little outside our box. Before the fourth session of the meetings, they asked if they could take the church on an "encounter" with God. Now, I want you to understand something important. They didn't just decide to do the encounter, they asked first. They were very honoring and would not have done anything out of order or without checking with those in authority in our house. As the senior leader of the church, it was clearly within my right to say I'd rather not if I didn't think it was good for our congregation. Too often we confuse awareness of what the Spirit can do with permission to do it. As a result, there are many people who have become wary of spiritual things.

I had personally experienced some "encounters" while in Redding at some of the conferences I attended but they had taken place with smaller groups who were being ministered to by Bethel's amazing team of supernatural intercessors. But I had never seen anything like what the student team wanted to do being done in a large church service. Not only were there many people from our own church present (and I wasn't sure all of them would be ready for this experience), but we also had many visitors who were already being stretched by all of the other manifestations of God's presence that were taking place. Needless to say I had a tiny bit of apprehension. (Yes, another word for fear.)

On top of my "concern" for those in attendance, I had some personal "questions". While I had seen many people benefit greatly from some of these types of encounters, I myself had not had much significant breakthrough during one of these experiences. Usually, I would just relax, enjoy a quiet time and then listen as others told of their amazing journeys into the presence of God. For me, however, there had been times when I came away a little disappointed. My apprehension was fueled by the idea that if I, as the leader of the church, didn't have some significant experience, it might have a negative impact on the people of our church. So, the truth is, when the team asked to do the encounter, it scared me just a little. But in spite of everything I was feeling, I knew that this could be a time of significant breakthrough for many and, therefore, it was not a time to draw back.

As we told those present what we were going to do, one of the team members began to play gently on the piano. The lights in the room were turned down and we were encouraged to make ourselves comfortable, some in pews, some on the floor. We closed our eyes as another team member began to encourage us to start asking God to take us to a special place where He could spend time with each of us. During each part of the "encounter" we were prompted to let God show us things. I was doing my best to be cooperative but for the most part I felt that the things that I was "seeing" were all just my imagination. I had heard the amazing testimonies of others following similar experiences but nothing I was feeling in that moment seemed at all powerful.

Then the speaker asked us to ask God for a new name. "What does He call you?" she asked. As I listened for God to say something, anything, I heard the name Aloysius. "Wow," I thought, "my imagination is really not cooperating now." It was almost as if my imagination were making fun of me. To me, the name Aloysius is a name you give to a child who you want to see get beat up after school every day for the rest of his life. I was thinking, "God, You wouldn't call me something that goofy, would You?" And the whole time I was lightly laughing at the silliness of the situation. Then God said, "Look it up!" I couldn't get up immediately because the encounter was still going on. So, I relaxed and waited. When the student team finished, I quickly grabbed my laptop and began searching online. (Our church has wireless access in the main auditorium so I was connected to the Internet in seconds.)

While I began to search, the team started asking people to come up and share their experiences. As I had seen before in past encounters, people began coming forward and telling amazing stories. If you heard them you'd know that their experiences were clearly real and if you knew some of the people (as I do) then you would be even more impressed. Often, the very people that you'd least expect to have any kind of positive result will come forward with extraordinary stories of being in the presence of God.

It took me a while to find the meaning of Aloysius because I had no idea how to spell it. While I was looking, I ended up listening to several different people share their encounters. Finally, I found it. When I did I was stunned.

As I said earlier, my idea of the name Aloysius was less than positive. I really don't know why I felt that way and for the record I want to say that if your name is Aloysius, forgive me, but for some strange reason, the name just didn't strike me as a name for a manly man. Initially, I felt as if God was calling me a sissy.

My parents named me Timothy (Honors God) Mark (Warrior) Hacker (German for wood cutter or woodsman). I've always loved the woods and hunted a great deal as a young man. I've also been a strong Christian since I was a young man and have always honored God. In recent days, however, I have felt the Holy Spirit encouraging me to take on more of the nature of my middle name, Mark, which means "warrior". I have even had some prophetic words telling me to be more of a warrior, confirming what the Spirit has been speaking to me.

So was God calling me a sissy? Not at all! Aloysius is of German origin and it means *famous warrior*. He was just reminding me of what he had already been telling me. I repent! (I see things differently!) I will never see the name Aloysius in the same way again.

God was doing more than just confirming who I am. He was also showing me that nothing about the "encounter" was just my imagination. If I were going to imagine a name for myself, I would have imagined something that I thought was cool; not something I thought silly.

I am so glad I didn't allow my personal fears to keep the church from experiencing this time of encounter. God is doing things in these days that many of us have never seen before. Past revivals have had some of the same manifestations but many of the manifestations look different in the 21st century. There are also some things happening that are unprecedented.

### What If?

Someone may ask, "What if these 'unprecedented' things you're doing aren't really of God?" The better question is, "What if they are?" Here are a couple of better questions: Is my relationship with God so fragile that it can't survive honest mistakes on my part? Is being led by the Holy Spirit so risky that we somehow think it better to possibly quench the Holy Spirit than take a risk?

The whole New Testament was unprecedented! "Yes, but the things that happened in the New Testament are in the Bible." Some will say. "If it's not in the Bible, then it's not of God!"

Really? Then the Amish are clearly more righteous than the rest of us! There are no cars in the Bible. No modern conveniences of any kind. Okay, I know I'm going overboard but I do so for illustration. Just where do we draw the line?

The Biblical church didn't have many of the things we have today. They didn't have buildings. They didn't have Christian education departments. They didn't have associate pastors, youth pastors, children's pastors, or any of a dozen or so other staff positions we have now. They didn't have a ton of stuff that Christians today can't do without. What they *did* have were signs, wonders, and miracles.

When it comes to what is and isn't in the Bible, allow me to challenge your thinking a bit. While everything in the Bible is of God, not all of God is in the Bible. How can I say that? It's easy! I can say it because the Bible says it.

At the end of the Gospel of John, we read, "*Jesus did many other things as well. If every one of them were written down, I suppose that even the whole world would not have room for the books that would be written.* (John 21:25 – NIV) Everything Jesus did was of God, but not everything Jesus did was written down. Therefore, all there is to know about God isn't in the Bible.

Yes, I know I'm scaring some of you. I'm sure the level of Xenophobia is rising up within some who are reading this. But stay with me. I'm not done yet. I'll probably make it worse before I make it better.

Try this little experiment sometime. Ask a group of believers if they read the Bible. You will no doubt get an emphatic, "Yes!" Then ask them if they have discovered anything new from the Bible in the last six months. I'll bet many if not most have. We've all had that experience of reading a familiar text when suddenly we see something we've overlooked before.

A great example in my life is connected to one phrase from the section of scripture most people call "The Lord's Prayer".

Not only had I read The Lord's Prayer many times but I grew up in a church that said it every Sunday. I had memorized it as a very young child and had repeated it thousands of times. I have led congregations in saying it hundreds of times and have taught on it many times as a pastor.

In 2005, in a meeting where Bill Johnson was speaking, I saw something for the first time that I had missed for nearly half a century. Bill simply pointed out that God had instructed us to pray that His will would be done on earth as it is in heaven. Then Bill asked the question, "Would God ask us to pray for something that He never intended to do?" It had never occurred to me that God would not ask us to pray for something unless He desired to do it. So, since we were taught to pray, "thy kingdom come, thy will be done on earth as it is in heaven", I suddenly realized that it was God's will to bring heaven to earth! I came out of the Jesus movement. Our paradigm was getting raptured and going to heaven, not bringing heaven here.

I'm sure many of you have read *When Heaven Invades Earth* by Bill Johnson. I am also as sure that I am not the only person that had said the Lord's Prayer thousands of times but didn't make the connection. I used to pray unsure of God's will. Now, I realize that His will on earth is the same as His will is in heaven and if it you can't find it there, it's not His will for it to be here.

How is it that we can miss things in the scripture one time and then see them so clearly the next? The reasons we miss them are probably too numerous to explain but the reason we have any understanding at all is simple. We really know nothing unless the Holy Spirit *reveals* it to us. The Bible itself teaches us that the Holy Spirit is our teacher. *"But the Counselor, the Holy Spirit, whom the Father will send in my name, will teach you all things and will remind you of everything I have said to you."* (John 14:26 – RSV)

The Bible also tells us that without the Spirit, we cannot understand spiritual things. *"The man without the Spirit does not accept the things that come from the Spirit of God, for they are foolishness to him, and he cannot understand them, because they are spiritually discerned."*

(1 Corinthians 2:14 – NIV) We all know that there are people who study the Bible without being in a relationship with God. We also know that many of them do so to refute the very book they're studying. Without the Holy Spirit, the Bible becomes just another book.

## Beware of Christian Know-It-Alls

So think with me. Is there anyone who has *all* of the revelation that the Spirit has to give to us from the Bible? Is it possible that at times we could be depending more on *our* understanding of the Bible rather than the Holy Spirit's understanding of the Bible? It's been said that if we have a relationship with God that we fully understand then we have an inferior relationship with God.

I said all of the above to get to this question; which is more important, the Bible that helps us live according to God's purpose in this world or the Holy Spirit without which we cannot truly understand the Bible? *I'm not trying to lower our esteem for the Bible*, I'm trying to raise our esteem for the Holy Spirit!

Among many Christians, there is a much greater fear of the unknown in the area of the Holy Spirit than there is over the scripture. We love the *"line upon line and precept upon precept"* of Isaiah 28 but we fear *"The wind blows where it wishes, and you hear the sound of it, but cannot tell where it comes from and where it goes. So is everyone who is born of the Spirit"* of John 3. The Bible is so tangible but the Spirit is so, well, *spiritual.*

Some will say, "The move of the Holy Spirit is so dangerous!" Yes, it is dangerous, and so are those who move by Its power. Some will say, "People could get hurt! It's too risky!" Allow me to repeat the quote from Helen Keller at the beginning of this chapter; *"Avoiding danger is no safer in the long run than outright exposure. The fearful are caught as often as the bold".*

Which do we believe in more, the Holy Spirit's power to lead us, or the devil's power to deceive us? Someone else might say, "I trust in the Lord, it's men that I don't trust." Unfortunately, in an effort to not trust in men we end up trusting only in ourselves. We end up trusting in our own understanding, which is the most likely place for deception.

> *"Trust in the LORD with all your heart and **lean not on your own understanding;** in all your ways acknowledge him, and he will make your paths straight."* (Proverbs 3:5-6 – NIV, emphasis added) So, do we stand still until the path before us is clear and straight or do we step out trusting Him to *make* the path straight?

I've heard leaders caution that the move of the Spirit has caused trouble in too many churches. Really? So, churches that don't have unusual manifestations of the Spirit have less trouble than those that do? That's silly. There are probably fewer churches in the U.S. that consider themselves "Spirit-filled" than there are that do, but it's pretty hard to find churches that don't have trouble from time to time. Do you know why? It's because all churches have people in them. And as Bugs Bunny once said, "Humans are the craziest peoples."

### Fear and Change

A fear that goes hand-in-hand with Xenophobia is Metathesiophobia, the fear of change. Change has caused more church wars than any doctrinal debate in history and anyone who has pastored a church knows what I'm saying is true! There have been times over the years of my ministry when it seemed like all the people around me had read, *"...I am the Lord, I change not..."* (Malachi 3:6 – KJV) and decided somehow that in order to be godly people (like God) they needed to resist change!

These people weren't evil people. They were just normal people. Change brings the unknown and change can be scary. Listen to these words spoken by Job:

> You renew Your witnesses against me, and increase Your indignation toward me; **changes and war** are ever with me. Why then have You brought me out of the womb? Oh, that I had perished and no eye had seen me! (Job 10:17-18 – NKJV emphasis added)

Job seems to be saying that the two worst things in life were war and change. Most people are familiar with the "horrors of war" but is change somehow just as horrific? If you too hate change, there are scriptures that seem to indicate change is not a good thing. (Check out Psalm 15:4 and Proverbs 24:21)

Scripture also recognizes that change is NOT easy.

> Can the Ethiopian change his skin or the leopard its spots? (Then) may you also do good who are accustomed to do evil? (Jeremiah 13:23 – NKJV)

People have established doctrinal stands on less scripture than I have given here! Yet, I would declare to you that God loves change. He is the God of changed hearts and changed lives.

Can his mercies be *"new every morning"* without waking up to change? (Lamentations 3:23) Can we *"grow up in all things"* without a change in our level of maturity? (Ephesians 4:15) Can we be *"instant in season and out of season"* without a willingness to experience change? (2 Timothy 4:2) How can we be transformed *"from glory to glory"* without moving out of an old glory into a new one? (2 Corinthians 3:18)

This all brings up another related fear, Neophobia, the fear of new things. New things bring change. Change brings the unknown.

Let's consider one of the most controversial areas of church ministry today, church music. In the last few years church music has become a huge area of controversy in churches in America. Consider these excerpts from letters sent to pastors:

> *"I am no music scholar, but I feel I know appropriate church music when I hear it. Last Sunday's new hymn – if you can call it that – sounded like a sentimental love ballad one would expect to hear crooned in a saloon. If you insist on exposing us to rubbish like this – in God's house! – don't be surprised if many of the faithful look for a new place to worship. The hymns we grew up with are all we need."*

> *"What is wrong with the inspiring hymns with which we grew up? When I go to church, it is to worship God, not to be distracted with learning a new hymn. Last Sunday's was particularly unnerving. The tune was unsingable and the new harmonies were quite distorting."*

The first excerpt was sent in 1863 to a pastor concerning the song, *Just As I Am*, and the second was written in 1890 concerning the song, *What a Friend We Have in Jesus*. As you read the letters did you think that they came from someone from this century? I thought you might.

I find it amazing that people of the **New** Covenant, who have experienced a **new** birth and a **new** life, and are walking in a **new** and living way carrying a **new** hope to the world can so easily find themselves longing for *"that old time religion"*. Again, don't get me wrong. I highly value the unchanging truths of our faith but most church battles have majored on the minors of function rather than the things that have eternal value.

### A New Song

Music is a perfect example. Nine times the scripture admonishes us to sing a new song to the Lord. Not once does it suggest that we should sing an old one. It's not that I believe that the old songs are of no value. Nor do I think that the Lord feels that way. What I do know is this; God is a creative being. His creative nature is in His creative people, like musicians. Creativity, by its nature, does something new. When someone does the same thing over and over we don't think, "Wow! That's creative!" A creative musician will naturally (or supernaturally) write a new song with a new melody and new words.

Another important aspect of music is that it expresses the heart. People write songs about what they are experiencing. People who are in a similar place in life connect with the songs that relate to those experiences.

New songs have accompanied every move of God in history. Why? It's because revival brings in new people who can't help but write songs about their new experience. They naturally sing about what God is doing, not about what He has done. They sing about their destiny, not their history.

I was in my office working on a new song for our worship team a few years ago when an older gentleman who attended our church at the time walked into my office. He said, "What are you working on Pastor?" When I told him I was working on a new song he responded, "Well, don't forget to sing the old ones too." I shared my thoughts about music and new songs with him and he smiled and nodded his head but I could tell it just wasn't sinking in.

After he left, I went out to see Joan, my secretary. Joan is an amazing person. At the time of this writing she could retire but she hasn't because she loves what she does.

Joan is actually a few years older than the gentleman who wandered into my office that day so when I went out to see her after his visit, I asked her what she liked better, the old songs or the new ones. Without hesitating she responded, "The new ones!" Joan is a revivalist! Her heart, even at retirement age, is focused on where God is going, not where He's been.

## Avoiding Controversy

If it makes sense to avoid things like the move of the Holy Spirit or fresh forms of worship in our churches in order to limit church divisions then what's next, our Bibles? It's my experience that Christians have fought more over what *they believe the Bible says* than they ever will over moves of God's Spirit.

The reality is that God's people would have less problems overall if we all would boldly pursue being **more** Spirit led. Think about it, how can we follow Paul's admonition to be led by the Spirit while avoiding the experiences we can only have through encounters with that very same Spirit?

The lack of esteem for the Holy Spirit among many of God's people has held back much that God is longing to reveal in and through His people. The good news is that God is beginning to change that lack of esteem. Believers everywhere are hungry for the greater level of relationship that comes through an intimate connection to God's Spirit.

As we establish greater levels of intimacy with God by His Spirit and strengthen ourselves by His Word, we will become more and more powerful in establishing His Kingdom on *"earth as it is in heaven"*. And what will that look like? I don't know completely. Much of it is **unknown**. That is why we should not, we MUST not be afraid of new, changing and unknown things.

Just remember, God has not revealed it all to us yet. For those of us who are afraid of the unknown, we can and we must "STOP IT!" The unknown was not intended to frighten us. It is intended to be a great adventure!

# Chapter 10

# Achievemephobia – The Fear of Success

*Success comes from knowing that you did your best to become the best that you are capable of becoming.*

*-- John Wooden*

There are so many phobias that this book hasn't addressed directly. As I mentioned earlier, with over 500 phobias known to exist, this book could be very, very long. If I am to be "successful" in my goal for this chapter, I will make this the shortest chapter in the book and you will be finished soon. Still, there is this one last phobia I wish to address.

The fear of success is a very strong fear. It almost seems as if some people are allergic to success. They get close to succeeding and then they self-sabotage just in time to rescue defeat from the jaws of victory. Almost all of us have experienced this at one time or another.

So, ask yourself, do I really believe I can succeed? Is it OK for me to succeed?

I believe that one of the biggest reasons we fear success is connected to an issue with our identity. If we have experienced some kind of bondage in our lives we will not see ourselves as having value and, therefore, we will subconsciously resist success. There are two categories in the area of identity bondage that I want to focus on here, captives and prisoners.

Captives are people who have been brought into bondage by the actions of others. They have become victims and will often identify themselves in that way. In times of war, innocent people are often captured and then confined though they themselves did nothing to deserve what they are experiencing. Today, there is a battle in the spirit realm over each of our lives and most, if not all, of us have been victims at one point or another.

Prisoners, on the other hand, are people who have done something wrong and have, by their own actions, brought themselves into a level of imprisonment. Shame and guilt have affected their identity and created labels under which they are forever limited in their own minds. Here is the Good News; Jesus came to bring freedom to both the captive and the prisoner!

> *The Spirit of the Sovereign LORD is on me, because the LORD has anointed me to proclaim good news to the poor. He has sent me to bind up the brokenhearted, to proclaim freedom for the **captives** and release from darkness for the **prisoners**.* (Isaiah 61:1 – NKJV emphasis added)

This was the portion of scripture that Jesus quoted in Luke chapter 4 when He announced the beginning of His ministry. It doesn't matter to God whether you are a captive or you are a prisoner, He just wants you to experience the freedom for which you were created.

If you have been a captive, you have been told over and over that slavery is your lot in life, your destiny. As has been said before, if you believe the lie you empower the liar. You are who God says you are. Your identity is found in Him, not in the circumstances you have experienced in life.

If you are a prisoner, you may be thinking that you don't deserve to experience the glorious freedom that Jesus died to provide. You're right, you don't. None of us do. That's what makes it so glorious! Your identity crisis has created in you the idea that you deserve freedom less than others because of some failure on your part. But again, you are who He says you are, not because of what you have done, but because of what He has done.

No matter what your situation, Jesus has a plan for you to break free from all fear and bondage and become successful. If you have been convinced (either by yourself or others) that you cannot or should not succeed, then it is now time to deal with the fear of success and enter into the destiny God has for you.

## Christians and Success

While doing research for this chapter I noticed something very interesting among the many quotes that I read. Very few success quotes come from Christian sources. Wouldn't experiencing the abundant life Jesus said He came to provide mean that Christians should be experiencing more success than any other group on the planet?

Success is almost a dirty word for far too many Christians. They seem to think that if they do anything great they might somehow get credit that they don't deserve and, as a result, rob

God of His glory. So first, let's settle one thing; God wants each of us to have a level of glory. How do I know this? Simple. You cannot give glory to God if you have no glory to give. And the greater the glory you have, the greater the impact you will have on the world around you when you give that glory to Him.

There is also a sinister and silent aspect to the fear of success. Often, because this fear is not even recognized, it masquerades as humility and is looked upon as a virtue. In an effort to avoid pride, we back away from things that make us feel celebrated. This can then lead to contempt for those who are celebrated and successful. I have often seen "celebrity" Christian leaders distained by fellow believers. Yet these same "Christian" people then wear the jerseys of their favorite secular sports figures. They feel comfortable celebrating the secular but not the sacred.

Consider the two following portions of scripture:

*Therefore humble yourselves under the mighty hand of God, that He may exalt you in due time.* (1 Peter 5:6 – NKJV)

*But seek first the kingdom of God and His righteousness, and all these things shall be added to you.* (Matthew 6:33 – NKJV)

We are universally celebrated as we *"humble ourselves"* and *"seek first the Kingdom"*. But, when *"in due time"* we experience being *"exalted"* and begin to have things added to us, many of our fellow Christians will "become concerned" that we are moving dangerously close to "worldly" success.

If we have an underlying sense that success is dangerous, then we will be afraid to succeed. We may even turn Achievemephobia into a badge of honor, choosing to embrace this fear as if we were pleasing God. But as I have said before, what you tolerate will eventually dominate.

Never get comfortable with any fear. A little fear tolerated is like a small leak in a dam; it is a sign of the flood that will ultimately come if it is not dealt with. Fear is not your friend. It is not your nature. It is not normal no matter how common it may be around you and no part of your identity should ever be based in fear. God has graciously allowed you to be able to sense fear so that you can be aware of danger and take action to stop evil. We must never, ever, forget that all fear must be vanquished so His Kingdom of love can be established.

## Stopping Fear Is Simple

While I believe that stopping fear is a simple act of repentance (changing the way you think), I have never said it would always be easy. In the year 2000 I heard a guy on the radio state that the best way to overcome halitosis was to brush the back of your tongue. I KNEW I could NEVER do that. My gag reflex was just too strong. Within a few days I heard about this simple cure again. I had always struggled with my breath. If I could just use this simple method I knew I would love the results. Then I saw another article about it and saw someone talking about it again on TV. I was seeing it everywhere.

Being a pastor, I have a lot of opportunities to pray with people and those prayers, more often than not, put me in very close proximity to people's noses. If I lay hands on someone and they go out under the power I want the "power" to be the Holy Spirit, not my breath! There had been too many times when my wife had come up to me sweetly offering me a mint but also making me aware that the last person I spoke to had likely been less then blessed by my breath.

So, though I KNEW that it wouldn't be easy, I decided to try something simple. The results on my breath were immediate. Brushing my tongue really worked! Gagging myself every morning was no fun but not worrying about my breath seemed worth it. I gagged myself almost every day for five years. Then, somewhere in the year 2005 I noticed that I wasn't gagging anymore. The simple thing had finally become easy.

Stopping fear really is a simple choice. Once you make the choice and begin to change the way you think, fear has already lost. Fear may go kicking and screaming but it will go. The Holy Spirit, which you have been given, is not a spirit of fear. He is the Helper and He will help you break through the darkness of every fear to experience the success He has always intended to be yours. When it comes to fear, you can "STOP IT" because you can do all things through Christ who strengthens you! (Philippians 4:13)

*Holy Spirit, thank You for the fear-free life of this reader. Thank You that they are ready, willing and more than able to defeat every fear and fully live in the freedom of Your love. We declare this truth in the mighty name of Christ Jesus our Lord. AMEN!*

Made in the USA
Charleston, SC
08 November 2013